M000158325

WARNING

This story discusses mental health issues and
suicide. If you or someone you know is affected
by any of the issues discussed, please seek help.
Call Lifeline any time on 13 11 14.
Or call Kids Helpline on 1800 55 1800.

Aboriginal and Torres Strait Islander readers are
advised that this book contains names and images
of deceased persons.

Important information: While this book is intended
as a general information resource and all care has been
taken in compiling the contents, it does not take account
of individual circumstances and is not in any way intended
as a substitute for professional medical or psychological
advice, diagnosis or treatment. It is essential that you
always seek advice from a qualified health professional
if you suspect you have health problem. Any views or
opinions expressed in this book by the author are personal
to him and made without guarantee. The author and
publisher disclaim any liability in connection with the use
or reliance of the information contained in this book.

JOE WILLIAMS is a proud Wiradjuri First Nations Aboriginal man born in Cowra and raised in Wagga Wagga, Australia. Joe played in the National Rugby League (NRL) for many years before switching to professional boxing in 2009 and winning two welterweight championships, despite suffering severe mental illness. Joe currently spends his time between Australia and the United States, travelling across both continents delivering workshops and talks to inspire people to think differently about their mental health.

To my parents for raising me, loving me and guiding me.
To Courtney and my children –
you are everything to who I am and why I am.
To every person fighting their battle –
dig in, cling on to hope, things get better.
To every person who has ever lost anyone to suicide –
I hope you find healing.

DEFYING THE ENEMY WITHIN

Joe Williams

ABC
Books

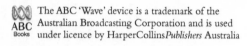 The ABC 'Wave' device is a trademark of the
Australian Broadcasting Corporation and is used
under licence by HarperCollins*Publishers* Australia

First published in Australia in 2018
by HarperCollins*Publishers* Australia Pty Limited
ABN 36 009 913 517
harpercollins.com.au

Copyright © 2018

The right of Joe Williams to be identified as the author of this work has been asserted
by him in accordance with the *Copyright Amendment (Moral Rights) Act 2000*.

This work is copyright. Apart from any use as permitted under the *Copyright Act 1968*,
no part may be reproduced, copied, scanned, stored in a retrieval system, recorded, or
transmitted, in any form or by any means, without the prior written permission of the
publisher.

HarperCollins*Publishers*
Level 13, 201 Elizabeth Street, Sydney NSW 2000, Australia
Unit D1, 63 Apollo Drive, Rosedale, Auckland 0632, New Zealand
A 53, Sector 57, Noida, UP, India
1 London Bridge Street, London, SE1 9GF, United Kingdom
2 Bloor Street East, 20th floor, Toronto, Ontario M4W 1A8, Canada
195 Broadway, New York NY 10007, USA

A catalogue record for this book is available from the National Library of Australia.

ISBN: 978 0 7333 3875 5 (pbk)
ISBN: 978 1 4607 0904 7 (ebook)

All photos courtesy of Joe Williams and family with the exception of: p 27 Darren
England / Newspix; p 47 Brett Costello / Newspix; p 66 Phil Hillyard / Newspix;
p 69 Gregg Porteous / Newspix; p 77 Sylvia Liber / Fairfax; p 105 Keith Abigail /
Rockfingrz; p 109 Addison Hamilton / Fairfax; p 148 Kennedi Sembiring;
p 163 Creek & Berry Photography.
Cover design by Darren Holt, HarperCollins Design Studio
Front cover image by Sunny Brar; back cover image courtesy of Joe Williams
Typeset in Bembo Std by Kelli Lonergan
Printed and bound in Australia by McPherson's Printing Group
The papers used by HarperCollins in the manufacture of this book are a natural,
recyclable product made from wood grown in sustainable plantation forests. The fibre
source and manufacturing processes meet recognised international environmental
standards, and carry certification.

CONTENTS

PART 2: DEFYING THE ENEMY WITHIN

First Steps

CONTENTS

FOREWORD

By Johnny Lewis, International Boxing Hall of Fame Inductee

I first heard the name Joey Williams after my good friend Brian 'Chicka' Moore returned to Sydney from Wagga and told me about a trial match he'd gone to between his beloved Newtown Jets and the Wagga Magpies.

A former rugby league champion himself, Chicka is a highly regarded judge of football talent, and I remember him saying, 'Johnny, you wouldn't believe this kid I saw on the weekend. He played against our first-grade team, and he played really well for a kid. I reckon he has enormous potential.'

Chicka told me he'd found out the young kid was the son of a former Winfield Cup player, Wilfred Williams, and he thought that might be why the kid had some decent potential. Back in the day, Wilfred had played in the Winfield Cup in a team coached by another great friend of mine, the legendary Arthur Beetson.

Anyway, Chicka went on to describe how after the game he'd gone into the dressing rooms to chat with this young kid, called Joey Williams. With a laugh, he recounted how after he'd said to young Joey, 'You went well tonight, son. What are you doing this week?' Joey's answer was, 'I'm going to school. I just started high school.' This both shocked and amazed Chicka.

Young Joe Williams was the tender age of thirteen when Chicka saw him that day, yet he was playing and dominating men who were fresh out of junior representative sides and lower-grade ranks of the National Rugby League (NRL). Chicka knew there was something special about this kid.

When Joey burst onto the scene in the NRL competition at twenty years of age, I could see what Chicka had been talking about. As well as having great skill and ability, Joey had a maturity beyond his years. It was during his first year in the NRL that Joey and I initially crossed paths in a local coffee shop in Erskineville, when he came over and started talking to me, not about footy but about his love of boxing.

I kept an eye on Joey from a distance over his initial few seasons and, like many others, I could see there were some inconsistencies in his on-field form. There were days when he was unstoppable and the best player on the park; other days you could hardly tell he was out there. One minute he'd be on top of the world and in the first-grade team, the next he'd be back in reserve grade. Being fairly observant, especially with regard to athletes, I put this down to a lack of experience, though I also thought something might be going on behind closed doors that was affecting his performances.

One day Joey phoned me out of the blue and said he'd heard I'd been doing a bit of extra fitness work with his teammate, Jaiman Lowe. He asked if he could come in to the gym to increase his fitness and help with his confidence — both of which boxing can provide. I thought it'd be perfect because as well as helping with his fitness I could work on his mental ability so he could be more consistent with his football week in and week out.

What young Joey Williams didn't realise was that I'd already had quite a few dealings with his old man, Wilfred, as well as many of his other Williams' relatives from Cowra.

When Joey started coming down to the gym at Woolloomooloo PCYC, it was about a quarter of the way through the 2007 season. Though his team, the Bunnies, had got off to a great start to the season, they were going through a rough patch.

I started off with Joey like I did with any other boxer who came through the doors — some chitchat, and then a little bit of boxing endurance to test his stamina — not only physically but also mentally. Like just about every single Aboriginal kid I'd had dealings with, Joey was a natural boxer. I've always said Aboriginal and Torres Strait Islanders are the most gifted athletes on the planet, and in the glimpses of rugby league talent I'd seen in Joey and just watching him swinging a few punches, I could tell the kid was a talent.

Joey kept coming to the Woolloomooloo gym and then to the Redfern PCYC when I moved there. We continued to work on his fitness and confidence, and he managed to gain selection back in the first-grade Bunnies' team and have a ripper of a finish to the 2007 season. The next year he moved very briefly to the Penrith Panthers and then to the Canterbury Bulldogs, but in the dealings we had together in

2008 I could see he was losing interest in the game he'd grown up loving.

I would continually ask questions of Joey and test his physical and emotional resilience during the training we were doing on the pads, and if I had a fighter getting ready for a bout who needed some rounds, I'd ask Joey. He was always up for it and passed the test, giving as good as he got. There were times he was tested to the point where he was knocked to the ground — but he always got up and came back for more.

At the end of the 2008 season, Joey decided he wanted to take boxing more seriously and committed himself to doing all he could in his preparations to become a boxer. After a while, we locked in a date for his first fight and increased his preparation. Watching Joey during that time was a treat. He walked into the gym with a reputation for not being a great trainer, but he soon blasted that talk out of the water, transforming his chunky 82-kilogram rugby league physique to 68.8 kilograms for his first professional fight. You don't shed over 10 kilograms by being lazy.

Joey went on to win twelve of his sixteen professional fights as a boxer, and I believe he could have gone on to even greater heights. But we weren't really trying to make him the champion of the world, we were building a resilience and mental strength to help him get through much greater battles.

I trained Joey Williams for his first three professional fights before moving back to the country, but I believe I gained a friend forever.

Sydney, 2017

NGINHA-LA-GU BA NGAPHI

(This Is My Journey)

Phalang ngiyanhi dumbarra yindyamarra, Ngiyanhi gingu mudyigaan, Marra dhalbu yaala (Today we show respect to the Elders past and present). When I was a young Aboriginal kid growing up in country New South Wales, I had a lot of ability at sports and was fortunate to excel at rugby league. I was only thirteen when I started playing representative schoolboy football as well as in weekend club competitions with much older blokes. By the time I was seventeen, I moved to Sydney to finish school and fulfil my dream of playing in the National Rugby League competition.

In my early twenties, I wasn't going so well with my league and took up boxing to increase my fitness.

I ended up liking boxing so much that I gave up playing league and became a professional boxer, winning a couple of titles to my name.

If I'd reached my full potential in either league or boxing, this might have been a book about my triumphs and successes in the sporting arena. But it's not, because as I entered the prime years of my life I was cut down by alcoholism and drug addiction, which stopped me from reaching anything like my full potential.

I was extremely fortunate to overcome my alcohol and drug abuse before they destroyed my life, but once all the substances I was using were taken away, *boom*, I had to face the head noise and paranoia I felt. I was swinging between manic highs and low depression. When I was really hyped or manic, I generally experienced positive dialogue. But when I was depressed, the dialogue was negative. It's what I now call 'the enemy within' — the voices in my head constantly questioning every decision that I make, telling me I'm worthless, even that I don't deserve to live, that I should end it all now.

When I was eventually diagnosed with bipolar disorder, I realised I'd been using alcohol and drugs to try to fight those mental demons.

I continued to have ups and downs with my mental health until a combination of a relationship crisis and not taking my medication for bipolar disorder pushed me to such a point of despair that I attempted to take my own life.

After my suicide attempt, I was thrust into discovering how to not only survive, but thrive. Over the years since, I have learned that I need to manage my life by always taking my medication as well as maintaining certain positive practices, which I've developed into what has become my 'wellness plan'. I've also gained a lot since learning more about my Indigenous culture and have become a proud Wiradjuri First Nations man.

Then, a few years ago, I participated in a short film called *The Enemy Within*. The documentary tells the story of how I managed to get back on top of my life through boxing, which taught me mental toughness.

That film has helped me deal with the really dark times. These were all things that had happened as part of my life, but to see it scripted reiterated to me that I'd been doing something that worked, and other people realised it too! It allowed me to relay my messages of inspiration to many different communities all over Australia and now internationally, communities where people suffer from or are exposed to friends and family with mental illness. Messages such as if you can't walk then crawl, but whatever you do, keep moving forward. The 1-per-cent efforts throughout every day are important, and every great person in life had to start somewhere.

One of the reasons why *The Enemy Within* spoke to people was that most of us don't want to talk publicly about mental illness or suicide. So many people reached out to me, over social media and in passing on the street, and it made me realise just how many of us are struggling in silence behind closed doors.

Pretty much anyone looking for inspiration or hope in relation to mental health can relate to the film. It's not because my story is the same as everyone else's, but because, while my life looked fine on the outside, behind closed doors I was struggling mentally and with substance abuse, just like so many others. I was helping to normalise the conversation about mental health.

I have since taken The Enemy Within project on the road to present in schools, youth and juvenile justice centres and to adults at corporate events.

Wanting to spread my message even further, I set up a website and Facebook page, and I have now connected with tens of thousands of people in need of advice or just the odd word of hope to help pull them away from the dark shadows. I am very proud and humbled that people feel confident enough to talk to me and trust me to be able to guide them out of their troubled times.

Doing this work on a full-time basis helps me to manage my mental illness by helping others. I feel extremely lucky to be alive and to be able to help so many others stay alive.

A large proportion of my time goes to helping our First Nations communities with mental health issues and suicide prevention. Recent statistics about suicide in Australia reveal that First Nations men in Australia between the ages of fifteen and thirty-five have the highest suicide rate in the world. This hurts my heart as I know I was nearly one of those statistics. There is much work to be done, and I believe an important first step is to implement programs that empower communities to revive our traditional culture. Far too often, non-Indigenous organisations try to deliver what they believe is the answer to a more positive way of life for Indigenous Australians with limited success.

Regardless of my achievements in league and boxing, I sincerely believe my journey with The Enemy Within will be my biggest and most significant contribution. Saving lives and impacting on individual people's mental health and wellbeing has a tremendous attachment to my heart, and I see my work now as being much more important than any sporting success. Which is why I wrote this book. Because I know that the only way I can have a positive impact and help others is by being honest and telling my story — both the good and the bad. I think the toughest part for me will be when my children read this book — they know my story, but this goes a little deeper. I just want to break down the barrier to help others seek help.

I haven't always been a winner, but by showing where I went wrong and describing how I dealt with my demons in this book, maybe you can be.

PART 1

MY STORY

1

MY WIRADJURI ROOTS

I grew up in Wiradjuri country, which encompasses the lands in New South Wales, Australia, that are the traditional home to the First Nations Wiradjuri people. I was born in the town of Cowra, one of five kids belonging to Wilfred and Lee Williams.

My dad's father was also called Wilfred Williams, though most people called him Willie. Granddad was an Aboriginal man from what was then called the Brungle Aboriginal Station or Brungle Mission, near Tumut in New South Wales. He was over six feet tall with a wiry and lean, chiselled body. He was a bare-knuckle tent fighter who travelled around from town to town, fighting in tents to make a few quid in order to feed his family and have the odd drink with the boys. If he didn't win a fight, there'd be no drinks and no food for the family. As well as his tent fighting, Willie also played lead guitar in a local band, which might be why I love listening to and playing music.

After Pop married my grandmother, Nan Olive, they immediately started having children. Sadly, my granddad died young, leaving Nan Olive to bring up nine children. She was just twenty-nine. Nan would later have another child, a daughter, so she had ten children in all, and she lost two more partners after Pop Willie — John and Paul.

Pop Willie.

My dad was nine when his father died, and he had a very tough life growing up in Brungle. Dad always laughs about how he, his siblings and pretty much all Olive's grandkids, including me, took after her when it came to height (all of us being short). With me being closer to the ground than Willie's six foot plus some, height is something I wish I'd inherited from him.

People who knew my father when he was growing up talk about the strength and physical toughness he and his brothers had. I believe they have a lot to thank my Nan Olive for. The strength and mental resilience it would have taken her to raise ten kids must have been enormous. Dad often tells me stories about how Nan got into physical fights in order to protect her kids when the family moved from Tumut to Cowra.

Even though she lost her husband so young, as well as a daughter shortly after birth and Paul and two of her sons in the past few years, Nan Olive continues to smile and has a great sense of humour. Every time I make my way through Cowra, I make sure to knock on Nan's door for a yarn about the old days in Brungle and the many stories of the tough times and struggles the family went through.

I always love hearing Dad's stories of his youth, which make me understand why he is such a physically and emotionally tough man. There are stories of how, when Dad and his brothers — Arthur (deceased), Shane, Dennis (deceased) and John — were teenagers, they would sometimes have to stick up for the family in physical fights with men. At times you hear of 'fight to survive', and they were literally fighting for the survival of the family.

Dad showed great potential as a footy player from a young age, but he didn't take it too seriously. The way he tells it, when he was about eighteen years old, he was walking home with a few drinks under his belt. He walked past the local footy oval

At times you hear of 'fight to survive', and they were literally fighting for the survival of the family.

and decided to join in a game of touch footy. A man called Greg Fearnley saw Dad had potential and began to encourage and motivate him. Dad says that Greg was the one who started him on his rugby league journey. Someone believed in him.

Brungle Public School footy team: Dad (middle back row)
and Uncle Arthur (back left).

From then on, Dad played football and always
showed potential on the field. In 1984, when he
was twenty-four, he was selected to play for the
NSW Country Firsts team. The much-revered
Indigenous league player and later coach, Arthur
Beetson, recruited Dad to play for the Eastern
Suburbs Roosters in Sydney in the Winfield Cup
competition that was the forerunner to the National

Rugby League competition. Dad stayed in Sydney for two years, going on to play for the Western Suburbs and then St George before returning to the bush.

My mum, Lee, was one of four kids born to Nan Shirley, a Wiradjuri woman from Orange, and Pop Ron, a non-Indigenous man. From the stories I've been told, Nan Shirl was quite the larrikin and life of the party, while Pop Ron was an accomplished boxer and also a bit of a joker. I vividly remember visiting him during the final days of his life at the time I was playing NRL with the Rabbitohs. Despite being on his deathbed, Pop Ron looked across at me and said: 'I'm still good for a few rounds [of boxing] so don't think because I'm lying down in bed that you'll beat me.' So right until his final days on earth he was cracking jokes.

Mum had two sisters, Tania and Lisa, and a brother, Craig. She never really speaks much about her upbringing — just says that her parents were strict on discipline, that they had some tough times financially, but they got by because of their love and support for each other.

I am told Mum was quite the athlete when she was younger, holding athletic and a few swimming records that still stand to this day. She and her brother Craig (now deceased) had enormous talent as kids and were invited to train with Olympic gold medallist Dawn Fraser. Mum did so well at school swimming carnivals and inter-town district meets that one day, when she was to compete in the age group 50 metres or 100 metres freestyle, she was made to do butterfly to even out the race. What the

Dad learning music.

organisers didn't realise was that Mum was actually stronger and faster at butterfly than freestyle.

Sadly, when Nan Shirl died, Mum's younger sister, Lisa, was only sixteen, so Mum took on the mother role to Lisa and they are still very close to this day.

So you can see there are some strong people in my family, and I'm pretty sure some of that strength rubbed off on me.

2

GETTING BY ON FAMILY, SPORT, MUSIC AND LOVE

When Mum and Dad first met in Cowra, Mum already had a son — my brother, Mike — and Dad already had a daughter — my sister, Jessie. Back then, Dad was playing rugby league. If his team won, he'd have enough cash to buy a feed of takeaway Chinese, have a few drinks after the game and buy two dollars' worth of petrol for the car, so he'd try his guts out on the football field to get a decent match payment.

Once Mum and Dad got together, they had me and then my younger sisters, Jasmine and Aleesha.

When we kids were growing up in Cowra, things were often tough financially, with only Mum working at times. But while we didn't always have much money, which was sometimes tough for us as kids, we learned to be grateful for what we did have. No matter how challenging the financial situations our family faced, we always seemed to get by. Looking back, I think the reason for this is that through every difficult time we not only loved and supported each other, but we were also respected within the Cowra community.

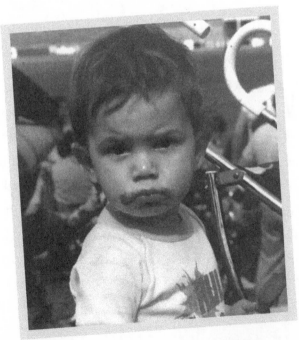

Little Joe.

Mum and Dad instilled strong values in us when we were growing up, and I still carry them with me as an adult. Even though there was never any money flashed around, we kids never went hungry or without the basics. Mum made sure we were well fed and well dressed. There were many occasions when Mum sat down to the dinner table with little or no food on her plate, which showed us the importance of thinking of other people before yourself.

Once, during my primary school days, I was in the school choir and had to wear a particular style of shorts and T-shirt for a performance we were doing. I knew our family wasn't doing great at the time, so I made up an excuse to the choir teacher about why I couldn't turn up so Mum wouldn't have to spend the money on the uniform. Little did I know that Mum had already gone out and bought the clothes that day. When I found out, I felt even worse because I knew Mum would have had to stretch our family budget to buy the clothes. I remember feeling so remorseful and sobbing to Mum about her having wasted money on clothes I wouldn't use. But as she always did with us kids, Mum just gave me a cuddle and told me not to worry.

There were also times when the ice-cream truck would drive up our street, music playing loud, with a dozen kids running behind it, waiting for it to stop. One day, every kid in our street was in the

Even when we were at fault, Mum still supported us.

line, even us — but then Mum put her head out the door and waved us back inside with a look of 'sorry kids, not today'. Those sorts of experiences taught us that we couldn't always get things just because we wanted them.

Mum was and is an extremely strong person and the rock of our family. To people who don't know her, she seems a fairly quiet woman but she's always good for a laugh and has a great sense of humour. She was amazing when it came to supporting us kids in any disagreements with others or when we needed help at school. Even when we were at fault, Mum still supported us, though sometimes when we got home she'd give us a kick up the backside for doing the wrong thing.

Then there was my brother, Mike. When I was growing up, I idolised and was in awe of him. For one thing, he was an amazing league player, which I wanted to be, too. When he was a teenager, scouts from rugby league clubs would travel to the country to watch Mike play, but if he got wind of it he would tell Mum he wasn't taking the field that day. He just had no interest in playing in the big league. Mike was a country boy and wasn't going anywhere.

Both being sports-mad, Mike and I were constantly battling for victory against each other, whether playing knee footie in the lounge room or cricket, rugby league or boxing outside. Sometimes when we were playing, Mike would wind me up to the point I'd end up running upstairs, my feet covered in dirt, crying out to Mum that Mike was cheating or being too rough. 'Don't go back down there if you can't handle it and don't come upstairs crying,' was always Mum's reply. Without fail, I'd go back for round two with Mike, often with the same result — me crying and running upstairs.

As Mike got older, I was the annoying little brother wanting to hang around him and his mates and getting the odd clip around the ear for trying to sneak into his room. I still admired him, though, and was in awe of how good a league player he was.

When Mike was eighteen, he was signed to play with the team Dad was coaching, Lake Cargelligo. Sadly, Mike only got to play one game because, after going into the sort of tackle he'd probably made a thousand times, he rolled with the opposing player, causing his forehead to be pressed close to his chest. After he jogged off the field, he walked over to our mother and said, 'Mum, I think I just broke my neck.'

Mike was right, he had broken his neck, and he was lucky not to end up a quadraplegic. The aftermath of Mike's injury was a terrible time for the family, and for a while Mum didn't want me to play league anymore. Her oldest son had just broken his neck, and she didn't want something like that to happen to me as well, and rightly so. But with time, Mum came to accept that Mike's injury was a freak accident, and she let me continue with my footy.

I would have backed myself against most people on the rugby league field, but before his accident Mike was lengths in front of me in all aspects of rugby league, something he occasionally jokingly reminds me of. He still lives in Cowra and is married with two lovely young daughters, Taniesha and Abbie.

Mount Austin Primary School, aged 11 — doing my best
to burst through.

My little sisters, Aleesha and Jasmine — or Leesh
and Jaye, as they are known to the majority of
people — had been born only a year apart. As kids,
Leesh and I would sometimes gang up on Jaye to the
point she would be running around the backyard
chasing us while we laughed and ran away. We had a
ball with it and still laugh about it. Despite Jaye being
the youngest in the family, we joke about how she's

the bossiest. I still remember one day when Mike and I were arguing with a group of boys who lived in our street, and three-year-old Jasmine came to support us holding up a slug gun. The police were called but Mum managed to bluff them by saying it was a toy machine gun.

To this day, Jasmine and Aleesha struggle when they haven't seen each other for a few days, and I only have to locate one sister to know the other isn't too far away. They have kids of their own now and, like me, they are applying the lessons from our upbringing in the way they parent. I am very proud of the way both of them have found ways in their life to improve their education and lifestyles. Jaye is a trained nurse who has worked within the mental health system as well with Dad in the area of juvenile justice. She gets on great with all the youth she deals with who have encountered obstacles in their lives that have led them into detention. She is raising two beautiful kids, Xavier and Xanthe.

Leesh was in a difficult relationship before she had her first two kids, Deminika and Elijah. I am very proud of her decision to go back to university to study teaching, despite the anxiety she feels at being away from home and her kids.

Top: Young and innocent — Leesh, me and JJ.
Bottom: JJ, me, Leesh — my face a little busted, after a fight the night before.

Despite always being very much part of our family, my older sister Jessie grew up living with her mother up at Erambie, the Aboriginal Mission community near Cowra. No matter how long it has been since we last saw each other, Jess and I always stay in touch and are still very close.

I've always had a brotherly relationship with my cousin Jason, who's the son of Mum's brother, Craig. We're still close and have plenty of laughs when we talk about things we did when we were growing up. When we were kids, we played footy on different teams, and when one of us was streaking away to score a try and saw the other in pursuit, we'd burst out laughing and almost drop the ball, which never went down well with the coach. Later, when we'd grown up and were both professional boxers, we found it hard to fight each other in training because we were always joking.

As you may know, many Aboriginal people have a huge extended family, both related and non-related, and we like to mix and mingle with each other. For as long as I can remember, we always had a close association with our extended family. When we lived in Cowra, we'd often catch up at barbecues that would go on from the brightness of a sunny afternoon into the darkness of night, playing and listening to music and chatting away. Sometimes when we got together we'd play rounders (like softball), but most of the time we'd play games of touch footy, which often lasted for hours with both laughing and arguments, due to people's competitive nature. Although I went on to play in the National Rugby League competition, I still remember the amount of skill my many cousins and friends showed back then.

As well as the barbecues, Mum and Dad sometimes went to or held house parties with family members and friends, where people would pass the guitar around the circle and take turns at singing a song. Growing up in a family where music was always present, I took to playing the guitar, and Dad would sometimes call on me to sing a song for the mob. Normally kids weren't allowed around the adults at house parties, but being able to belt out a few tunes was the one reason why I was allowed to stay and listen to the yarns of Dad and his friends. I found that singing in front of people at those parties helped me get over my shyness and gain more confidence. It also gave me a love of music from the 1960s, '70s and '80s and bands and singers such as The Eagles, Creedence Clearwater Revival, Sam Cooke and Otis Redding.

So, in those early years, we might not have had much, but we had each other, we had our extended family and we all shared a love of sport and music. These foundations gave me the strength I needed to get through some tough situations later in life.

JJ, Dad, Nan Ollie, Me, Leesh, Jessie and Mum.

3

GROWING UP FAST

When I was ten, Mum and Dad decided to move from Cowra to Wagga Wagga so Dad could take up a country football coaching job. Wagga was bigger than Cowra, and they thought it might also provide more opportunities for us. Before we left Cowra, Mum agreed that Mike could stay there and live with his father in order to continue working towards his apprenticeship. Jessie also remained with her mother at Erambie.

Located in southern inland New South Wales, Wagga was a great place to grow up. It had a decent population of Aboriginal people (who are called Kooris in New South Wales), and seemed to be a little more accepting of Indigenous folk than other places. Through his football and other things, Dad knew lots of different Koori families in Wagga so we were introduced to heaps of Koori kids when we arrived, which was great.

I enjoyed living in Wagga from the get-go. Our family was happy, I liked going to Mount Austin Primary School and there were lots of sports opportunities for me. It was in Wagga that I was introduced to representative sport for the first time, playing for the school in many different sports, which provided me with the chance to make even more new friends.

Even though I liked pretty much all sports, even as a primary-school kid I showed particular promise at rugby league. I'd grown up following the game, watching it on TV for hours and idolising players — my two favourites being David Peachey and Andrew Walker. The house we lived in when we moved to Wagga was across the road from the high school, and I would spend any spare moment I could running around and kicking a footy, trying to emulate NRL players, and even commentating on my own moves.

In 1995, when I was twelve, I was the first person from the Riverina to captain the New South Wales primary schools rugby league team. Not long after, I came to the attention of rugby league immortal

Captain of the NSW Primary Schools Sports Association
rugby league team — 12 years old, practising my signature.

and Indigenous legend Arthur Beetson, who made
our family an offer for me on behalf of the Roosters.

Funnily enough, Arthur had also invited Dad
to play with the Roosters. Dad had been stuck in a
bit of a cycle of alcohol and mischief at the time. If
Beetso hadn't given him a chance to improve his life
by playing in Sydney, who knows what the future

would have been like for Mum and Dad? There's every chance Dad would have stayed in familiar surroundings and not challenged himself. As it was, Mum and Dad moved to Sydney and lived with Arthur for some time, and while Dad didn't play out his entire career with the Roosters, it was through Beetso that he learned the mental and physical toughness it takes to play at the top level.

Even after moving on to two other clubs in Sydney, Dad maintained a great relationship with Arthur, and would still hear from him when he was on his trips around rural and regional New South Wales and Queensland, scouting for the next schoolboy prodigy. Artie was remarkably successful at recruiting players, with many guys he'd picked going on to play top-grade NRL, State of Origin and even for Australia.

Some other league clubs had contacted Mum and Dad about me playing for them before Arthur approached us. But Mum was adamant that getting an education was far more important than throwing a football around and believed I had the potential to be more than just a footballer. 'I don't care about how much money a club promises my son,' she said to Arthur. 'The club that's prepared to give Joe the best education will get his signature.'

After that, the focus of the negotiations changed. It wasn't so much about the money anymore, but about providing me with a scholarship to a good school. Ultimately, when the offer was put on the table, it included covering any private school fees. So at the age of thirteen I signed my first NRL contract.

There is no way my parents would have been able to afford a private school education, so thanks to Mum I was lucky enough to go to St Michael's Regional Boys High School in Wagga from Year 7 to Year 10.

Arthur Beetson, an amazing man, travelled the country looking for young Aboriginal talent.

In my first year at St Mick's, I was invited to play with the older students in representative teams and was named player of the final in a state-wide competition for two years in a row.

Outside of school, the next year I was due to go into the Under 14s, but my parents decided to let me play in the under 18s competition with the Wagga Magpies. Despite being so much younger than my teammates, I managed to play well all season, and our team made it to the grand final against the Gundagai Tigers. The Tigers had beaten us twice that year, and we were not expected to win the game. With two minutes on the clock, we were behind by four points, and the game was all but lost when we spoiled a chance. The Tigers were given the scrum feed, but it turned out that fate wasn't on their side that day. We won the scrum against the feed, the ball was passed out to me and I managed to step through a couple of defenders to score the winning try next to the posts.

By Year 9, around the age of fifteen, I was selected for the New South Wales combined Catholic Colleges' rugby league team, and was named captain. We were runners-up in the national competition, but I played well enough to be selected for the Australian

Under 15 merit team, and I still have the playing strip I was given.

Over the next few years I moved into the senior age groups and was selected to play halfback in the Australian schoolboys' representative team with players such as Greg Bird, Michael Weyman and many others who went on to play in the NRL system.

Having played high-level league in both the country and Sydney, then coached country teams, Dad was my toughest but smartest critic with footy because he knew what I was capable of achieving on the field. And when it came to trekking up and down the Hume Highway between Wagga and Sydney almost every weekend for representative games and practice during high school, it would be Mum driving me. As well as being extremely thankful for all the time she spent taking me backwards and forwards to Sydney, I also appreciated all the money Mum and Dad spent on me during this part of my football journey. To this day, I think of the things my brother, sisters and parents went without in order for me to chase my dreams.

Playing high-level rugby league at such a young age sometimes proved difficult. I was exposed to

Australian Schoolboys team. I am between Greg Bird and
Trevor Thurling, who would both go on to have sucessful NRL
careers. This was clearly before I understood the meaning of
the Australian national anthem.

drinking among the older players in my teams,
started experimenting with alcohol and began
hanging out with the wrong crowd. We'd train
hard during the week, then party hard after the
games. Next thing I'd be at a school-age party,
where I'd sneak in alcohol as if I was still hanging
around adults.

There were times I'd tell Mum and Dad I

was staying at a friend's house and instead walk the streets until the early hours of the morning, drinking and getting up to no good around the local neighbourhood.

I began to live a double life at school and around the community. I had a good reputation around town and within the school. I was trusted to go into the school canteen, pay and serve myself lunch. But there were times I took a little 'too much change' to buy alcohol on the weekend. I still feel deep remorse for the way I acted on countless occasions during those days. Looking back, I often wonder if my time playing higher-grade rugby league for Wagga back then was the catalyst for some of the addiction problems I faced later.

There was even a point where I got into sniffing petrol. I remember one afternoon I chose to stay home while Mum and Dad went to visit some cousins at their house. As soon as they left, I wandered out to the shed and buried my head deep in the lawnmower petrol can. I wasn't to know that Mum and Dad had decided to come home early, and when I heard them pulling into the driveway, I shot out of the shed, trying to look innocent. As it turned out, Dad had actually come back to get that exact petrol can. As he walked into the shed, he asked me if I'd been doing anything silly because of the strong smell of petrol. With my heart racing and my head clouded from petrol fumes, I denied I'd been doing anything wrong and told him the smell of petrol in the air was because I'd been thinking of starting some fires. That reply was even sillier than admitting to what I'd been doing.

What Dad said to me in response to my lie sank in more than any physical punishment. 'Joe,' he said, 'you have a decision right now about which road you decide to take in life. You can head down the path of destruction, drinking alcohol and taking drugs and other silly things — which we've seen many cousins and family friends do — or you can change your behaviour and chase your dreams of becoming a professional footballer.'

He then put his hand on my shoulder and asked me to look him in the eye. 'We'll support you as much as we can, but only you can decide how much you really want that dream.'

Dad's words rang home loud and clear, and I never went near a petrol can again. It was also around this time that I started to distance myself from the group of friends I'd been delving into negative behaviours with.

Despite all these difficulties, I always seemed to find a way to produce a big game when the team needed it the most, and we won most of our games.

Dad's words rang home loud and clear, and I never went near a petrol can again.

Looking back, I consider myself very lucky to have played in a grand final in almost every junior grade, often in teams laced with cousins and good friends.

My love for and commitment to rugby league was paying off. It looked like I had a bright future in the game, if I wanted it.

4

BLATANT RACISM

Until I started high school I only went to public schools, where I had lots of Aboriginal friends to hang out with. St Mick's had a hugely different demographic when it came to financial stability, and it was at St Mick's that I first experienced blatant racial discrimination.

During a schoolyard competition of basketball and touch footy, I was openly called 'a black c★★t', 'a coon' and 'a nigger', among many other discriminatory remarks. At first, I tried my best to brush it off, but being the only boy there identifying as Aboriginal, I knew I had to put a stop to it pretty fast. My parents had always told me to stand my ground when it came to bullying and most definitely racism.

One day I got into an argument with two guys

when one of their friends started to verbal me. This guy had been one of the few who'd been racially abusing me, and quite frankly I was sick of it.

The old man had always said to me: 'If you look like getting into a fight, make sure you let the first

My parents had always told me to stand my ground when it came to bullying and most definitely racism.

one go. Don't run the risk of being sat on your backside first.' So after a quick glance around for any teachers, I let this guy have three or four in the mouth. The scrap didn't last long — someone pulled me off the kid, who was down on the ground.

I was taken to the principal's office, and my parents were called. Staunch as ever, Mum supported me strongly because she knew I had been the victim of racism. The other kid ended up needing surgery on his mouth, and I got into a fair bit of trouble. I learned I was okay in a scrap, but I also learned that violence was not the answer when trying to sort out a disagreement.

A few days later, both sets of parents were called into the school because the other kid's father was demanding we pay the medical bills. He was sitting next to Mum in the office, and they got to talking. Mum is a fair-skinned woman, and the kid's dad mustn't have realised I was her son. 'I'll kill the little black bastard when I get my hands on him,' he said.

Needless to say, Mum let him have a fair share of her mind. She also let the school principal know that racism can have a big impact physically and emotionally on an Aboriginal child's life and needed to be dealt with. In the end, I was given two days' inter-school suspension. From then on, the other guy and his crew didn't come at me with racial remarks.

After that, Dad really hammered home the importance of not letting it affect me emotionally.

'So what should I do or say when somebody calls me a racist name?' I'd ask him.

'Son, if someone calls you a black c★★t,' Dad would say, 'well, you are black, so they are half telling the truth. So you tell them, last time you checked in the mirror you were black.'

He was right: 'black' isn't an insult. I am coloured, and I'd be disappointed if people suggested otherwise.

With Mum at my Year 10 school formal (bleached hair was big at the time).

Dad also told me to always stand my ground and never let racially vilifying words stop me from becoming the best person and the best leader for our people that I can be. If I let racial abuse weigh me down, he said, then the perpetrator won. If I didn't give the abuse energy, then I won instead.

But I did sometimes feel I was unfairly victimised during my junior rugby league days. I remember when I was playing Under 13s being physically shoved by the opposing coach, then being suspended for swearing in retaliation. I also received a six-week suspension for grabbing an opposing player by the collar and slinging him to the ground. It was an aggressive tackle, but the punishment was greater than the crime.

In my early teens, I became so discouraged by some of the treatment I received playing league that I almost switched to AFL. I did play a few seasons

Racism can have a big impact physically and emotionally on an Aboriginal child's life and it needed to be dealt with.

of AFL in the local Wagga competition because it was played on Sundays and rugby league was on Saturdays. Even though I was always drawn back to league, AFL helped me a lot with my general kicking ability.

Despite those early experiences of racism, I loved my time at St Mick's and met lots of friends from many different walks of life. I also formed friendships with some of teachers at St Mick's that have carried through into my adult years. When I later became an Aboriginal Education Worker, I worked with as many as a dozen of my former teachers from my St Mick's days.

After finishing Year 10 at St Mick's, I went to Trinity Senior College in Wagga for Year 11. Then, just after I turned seventeen, the time came for me to take the next step of my rugby league career and move to Sydney to start training with the Roosters. Arthur Beetson told Mum and Dad he was happy for me to live with him and his partner Anne and son Mark, and the Roosters organised a scholarship for me to go to Marcellin College in Randwick.

5

FROM THE BUSH TO THE BRIGHT LIGHTS

Moving to Sydney to chase my dream in the NRL was a fantastic opportunity, and spending my first two years in the big city under Arthur Beetson's roof gave me a lifetime of memories and was an experience I am truly grateful for. It was incredible to have the opportunity to live with and be coached by Beetso, and I knew I had to take in as much of his knowledge as I could. But those years also provided me with some of the biggest and toughest life lessons I've ever learned.

I'd originally planned to finish Year 12 in one year, but it was difficult to combine studying and trying to carve out an NRL career. So I elected to study for my HSC over two years through the Pathways Program.

During the 2002 pre-season, I got my first taste of mixing with the squad as a full-time player. I was expected to train with the team either on the field or in the weights room two or three times a day, five days a week. It was essential to get to training on time, but one day I was running late to a mid-morning session because I'd had to stay at Marcellin a bit later than usual for school photos.

I raced to training, knowing I'd get in trouble from coach Ricky Stuart for being late. Sure enough, being the tough coach he was, Ricky started ripping into me for not being on time.

When I told him I was late because I had my school photos, he and all the players burst out laughing. For the next few weeks, it became the running joke as an excuse for being late.

I learned so much during that off-season and impressed the coaching staff enough to be chosen in the top squad for the trial period. Having just turned eighteen, it was a pretty big thrill for a kid from the bush to be training and hanging out with first-grade players, some of whom were in the New South Wales and Australian teams. It was amazing to play in two trial first-grade NRL games at halfback inside Brad 'Freddy' Fittler, one of the greatest five-eighths of all time.

One day I still remember distinctly, I was playing with the first-grade Roosters team in a trial match against the Brisbane Broncos. As a halfback, one of my main jobs was to steer the team around the park, call the team plays and put us in the right positions on the field. As a young rookie halfback, it was a dream having Brad Fittler running outside me.

During this particular game against the Broncos, Freddy called out a direction to the team, and without thinking I screamed out an opposing directional call.

Freddy looked at me like, who's this kid telling me, 'No, we're taking a different direction?'

I froze in shock, having just gone against the orders of one of my childhood idols and the captain of the team.

To my surprise, Freddy called out: 'You heard Joey, that's what we're doing.' In saying those words, he acknowledged that directing the team around the field was my job, and he respected my call.

Speaking to him many years later, I asked him what he'd thought in that moment. He said he thought I might be feeling a little shy because I was playing with more senior players, so he jumped in to take over. As soon as he realised I knew it was my job to direct things and I wasn't shy about doing so, he respected that. We have seen each other over the years at various events, and I still greatly admire him.

I didn't make my NRL debut that year because the coaching staff wanted me to gain a little more experience playing in the Roosters' Under 20s NRL Jersey Flegg side. Looking back, although I felt like I was ready, I definitely needed the time and experience under my belt to become a more complete player and the sort of on-field leader a halfback needs to be.

At the time, though, it was disappointing to go from playing with the first-grade team one week to training with guys who were pretty much hoping to get a spot so they'd be contracted. This showed me the importance of humility, and was a reminder that I shouldn't get ahead of myself.

It was after I was put back to the Under 20s that I first noticed the negative voices in my mind rearing their ugly head, telling me I didn't deserve to be in Sydney at all given I wasn't playing first grade, and that I should just pack up and head back to the bush, because I was worthless.

Back then there wasn't as much emphasis on the psychology of professional athletes and the pressures that came with playing elite sport. There were days when training staff were almost like drill sergeants from the army. Sometimes they screamed at players and humiliated and even degraded players in front of other members of the team. Occasionally they would even bring the racial identity of a player into the abuse. It may be that they believed this was the way to make the players mentally stronger, and that if you weren't mentally strong you should just give up playing rugby league. For me and many others, that approach of ridicule, embarrassment and tough love didn't work. In fact, it had the opposite impact of sending my self-esteem lower and lower.

After a while, I started to hear voices in my mind telling me I wasn't good enough and didn't deserve to be playing in first grade. These voices got more constant, to the point I started to think I didn't deserve to be alive.

I would catch myself shaking my head or nodding even though no-one else was around, but I wasn't having a conversation with someone else — it was all in my own head. Sometimes the chatter would be positive on the rugby league field, when the voices ran through the plays before I did them. But the negative thoughts were a different story altogether. They'd often spiral out of control, to the point where I felt like I was witnessing an argument taking place

After a while, I started to hear voices in my mind telling me I wasn't good enough and didn't deserve to be playing in first grade.

between two separate people; the negative Joe and the positive Joe. The head noise and voices impacted on my mental wellbeing so severely that it started to affect me physically.

Things grew worse, as the voices wreaked havoc on my ability to think. I started second-guessing every decision I made both on and off the field. The voices became so vivid and loud in my head, it was like I was hearing actual voices. After a while, I became so anxious and down that I'd get to the point where I'd convinced myself I was worthless, a failure.

The combination of those negative voices with training staff telling me I was weak if I hadn't made a certain time in a run, or that I didn't deserve to be at that level if I didn't try harder, began to feel overwhelming.

I'm not sure if it still happens but, back then, if you didn't achieve what you were asked to do, you

I'd convince myself I would be dropped from the squad because of the negatives in my game.

were sometimes banished from the team — until you showed you deserved to be included. I remember one of the coaching staff blasting and ridiculing me in front of the team at halftime during a game because I was wearing white football boots rather than black. He ranted and raved at me, saying I had a poor attitude, among other things, and to take the boots off and throw them away. Fast forward five years and players were wearing white, bright orange and even pink boots.

Even on the days I didn't put a foot wrong on the footy field or won player of the match, I'd convince myself I would be dropped from the squad because of the negatives in my game. I would be scared to go to training because I dreaded the coach saying I wouldn't be in the team the following week. These

Kicking the winning field goal for the roosters in the Jersey
Flegg Grand Final. One of my close mates, Josh Cale, is watching
on. We knew it was going over as soon as it left the boot.
We joke that I stole his thunder by taking his shot at goal.

negative thought processes continued for the majority
of the year, getting so bad I often had to force myself
to turn up to training because I'd convinced myself I
didn't belong there.

The only way I knew how to combat these constant
thoughts, turn down the voices and deaden the pain I
felt was to drink as much alcohol as I possibly could.

And although on the field it looked like things were okay, I was battling behind closed doors.

Despite the negative voices and drinking, I managed to stay on track with my footy, even captaining the Under 20s Roosters team. They were a great bunch of guys and good players, and we ended up having a fantastic season and making it through to the grand final. On the day of the grand final, I kicked three goals, had two try assists and kicked the winning field goal. After our first-grade team also won their grand final, we had one hell of a party that went on for a few days.

6

THE TOP GRADE

During the 2003 season, I was really battling emotionally, suffering from homesickness and looking for comfort at the bottom of a bottle. I started partying more and drinking even more heavily, which I now realise was a bandaid solution for my mental battles. Instead of concentrating on playing well, I was busy worrying about what drinking and late-night partying the crew had planned for after the game.

It all began to take its toll physically and mentally. At the same time, I found I was clashing with some of the coaching staff. I began to lose interest in what I was doing and was no longer happy at the Roosters. I became desperate for a change. As a result, I decided to finish up at the Roosters at the end of the season and move to the South Sydney Rabbitohs.

When I called my mother to tell her I'd signed with the Rabbitohs, she burst into tears of joy. Mum had been an avid Souths fan since she was a young girl and had dreamed that one day she'd get to see me run out in the famous red and green South Sydney colours.

I'd signed with Souths to show I was still keen to be an NRL player, but the money wasn't great, so the pre-season was tough. As a result, I had to make a living like many league players did, working long hours labouring on a construction site doing hard physical work. Afterwards, I'd go to football training then get some sleep and do it all over again.

To make matters worse, I broke my thumb in the opening trial game and had to have surgery on it, causing me to miss the first six weeks of the season. That was really tough, but it made me realise I'd have to work much harder to even be picked for the reserve-grade team. Competition is always tough for the halfback position, so I needed to not only train hard to improve the physical aspect of my game but also to build up my mental toughness.

I started to do extras with my fitness and general game skills. I was no longer drinking so much or partying hard, as I didn't have much money. After a few weeks of putting a huge effort into training and committing myself both physically and mentally, I was picked in the reserve-grade team. I started to play myself into form, stringing a few good games together, and it was noticed by the coaching staff.

Around this time my partner, Suzie, who I'd met through a mutual friend, found out she was expecting our first child. Suzie and I had knocked

It all began to take its toll physically and mentally.

around the same touch footy circles and she was a great support to me in my early career, especially in my chase for the NRL dream. Because I wanted our child to be born into a financially stable environment, I started paying even more attention to my footy and didn't drink much. Week by week, as I put some great games together, I continued to impress the coaching staff, and it wasn't long before I was picked in the first-grade team to make my NRL debut. Finally, the time had come to live out my childhood dream.

I didn't sleep a wink the night before my first-grade debut. On the way to Shark Park, I seemed to take every wrong turn and was late for the warm-up. All the players laughed at me for being late and in a screaming mess. To my surprise and happiness, though, the coach had organised for my dad to present me with my playing jersey. This is a memory we both hold very close.

I was full of nerves and a rattling mess when I took to the field as an NRL player for the first time.

I didn't sleep a wink the night before my first-grade debut.

I'd dreamed of this moment for most of my life, and the fact I was playing for the mighty South Sydney Rabbitohs made things even sweeter.

People sometimes ask me what it was like playing my first NRL game. The funny thing is, I copped a knock to the head that gave me a mild concussion for the rest of the game. I do remember that we lost, but one thing that stood out for me was that my idol, close friend and mentor Dave Peachey, was playing in his 200th NRL game. After the siren and when we were shaking hands, 'The Peach' said to me: 'Young brother, as my career is nearing its end, yours is just starting. Good luck.'

I had spent my entire life chasing the dream of becoming an NRL player. I now had the monkey off my back, and it was time to get to work and live up to my potential.

7

DRUGS

Wins were few and far between for Souths in 2004. It was challenging, but nowhere near as difficult as what I was going through off the field. My alcohol abuse was becoming rampant again, now I was earning more, and playing first grade had sent my ego to an all-time high, especially after I was named Rookie of the Year 2004.

Things got even worse when I discovered party drugs during the 2004–2005 off-season. I'd smoked a little bit of marijuana in my youth, but nothing extensive. And since I read a book called *Anna's Story* about a teenage girl who died of an overdose of ecstasy, I'd been terrified about using party drugs, and had promised myself I would never go near any of the harder stuff. Little did I know where the next few years would take me.

As anyone who knew me during my early NRL days knows, I enjoyed being the life of the party, laughing and joking, the centre of attention. On Mad Monday, I celebrated by drinking so much alcohol I couldn't stand up. That afternoon, a guy I'd never seen before, who was partying with the group, approached me and asked if I needed anything to help me stay awake. That was the day I had my very first ecstasy tablet. Boom. I was instantaneously hooked.

That same afternoon, I had my very first line of cocaine. After I'd inhaled it, I looked up at a teammate who'd just done the same. A million things were going through my head. As much as I knew what I was doing was wrong, I also felt a euphoria like I'd never experienced before. I felt like a rock star in a packed Wembley Stadium, with all the lights shining on me. From that point on, as soon as any type of mind-altering substance entered my body, it set off a craving to keep going and going and not want to stop.

Drugs made me feel invincible, on top of the world. The more I had, the more I wanted — I didn't want the feeling of complete euphoria to end. I'd lose all control and feel as if I didn't have a problem in the world. During these euphoric moments, the voices in my head would disappear and it felt like nothing could bring me down.

I pretty much spent the rest of the 2004–2005 off-season in party mode, drinking and using drugs every weekend. My profile had grown since I began playing first grade, and I was recognised more in public places. It was quite normal to be shouted beer when I was out on the town at night, and be offered a line or two of cocaine.

Suzie was still pregnant, and we organised a holiday to her home town of Darwin. The weather there was so hot and humid, I used it as another

I enjoyed being the life of the party, laughing and joking, the centre of attention.

excuse to drink to excess. The more I drank, the messier I got, drinking until I vomited, then rinsing my mouth out with water and drinking more. Beer, spirits, cheap wine — you name it, I guzzled down anything I could get my hands on. I was so drunk when I arrived at Darwin Airport to head down to Sydney, I was almost refused entry to the plane.

At times like these, Suzie would be extremely embarrassed. As well, when I drank too much, I'd spend the money we needed to live on week to week. It all caused a huge strain on our relationship. And the more I drank, the more I took drugs, and the worse my thought patterns became, to the point where I would drink and take more drugs to shut them down. Round it went. By the beginning of 2005, my life was spiralling out of control.

It was during this crazy time that Suzie gave birth to our son, Brodi Ali Joseph Williams. I was on top of the world. When the *Daily Telegraph* ran a picture of Brodi and me on the front page, I remember saying: 'There have been terror attacks, Osama Bin Laden is at large, and they've got a little Koori boy from the bush on the front page.'

But it wasn't enough to make me change what I was doing, and as a result of all the partying, drinking and rubbish food I'd been eating for so many months, I had gained ten kilograms by the time I returned to training in 2005. The coaching staff weren't happy and, as a result, I was put into the 'fat club' — the name for the group of training players who'd come back from the off-season overweight. I worked hard in that pre-season and shed five or six kilograms, but focusing on losing weight meant I wasn't concentrating on finetuning my game or learning more. So, while I started the year in first grade, I was dropped to reserve grade after just eight games. I'd paid the ultimate price for coming back overweight. I also had a poor attitude towards everything I'd need to do to keep me on the field and playing well.

Of course, my relationship with Suzie was no longer in great shape. Not surprisingly, she wasn't very happy about all my late nights out and my excuses and lies about partying and drinking. I knew I was doing the wrong thing by both her and Brodi and that my life was heading down a dangerous path.

Being demoted from first grade really gave my ego a kick, and the negative chat between my ears started up again in force. My mind was a racing mess, and the only way I knew how to quieten down the constant negative banter in my head was to continue to drink and take as many drugs as I could. For some strange reason, I kept thinking the answers to my bad form on the field and my relationship troubles with Suzie could be found in alcohol and drugs. It was a vicious circle.

I couldn't go to the pub to have a quiet beer. Instead, I'd drink to excess and then go looking for whatever drugs I could get my hands on, whether it was a bag of cocaine, some ecstasy tablets or speed.

The more I drank, the more I took drugs, and the worse my thought patterns became.

I even used ice on some occasions. I liked to keep partying through the night and would often call in sick to training because I was too intoxicated from the previous night or coming down from heavy drug use.

One day, I missed a mid-week training session after going to an Oasis concert with a heap of school friends from Wagga. We stayed out for the majority of the night, and I got completely wasted. Another time I was so out of it I called my reserve-grade coach in a panic to explain why I was late for training. 'It's our day off,' he replied. I'd completely lost track of the days.

I'd gone from a kid who wanted nothing more than to be a successful NRL player to a lost young man with very little love for the game left, who gave more priority to going out at night than performing well on game day.

I hated the man I'd become. Yet the more my self-loathing increased, the more I would drink and take

I'd drink to excess and then go looking for whatever drugs I could get my hands on.

drugs. There were times I even went to bed with a skin full of drink and drugs, hoping to not wake up because I was convinced that the world would be better off without me.

My head was a mess, my priorities were all out of whack and I was heading downhill — fast. Although I knew I wasn't doing the right thing, I just couldn't be honest with myself enough to get help for my problems.

Someone suggested I turn to the church and ask God to help me with my alcohol and addiction problems. So, at the beginning of 2006, I decided to give it a red-hot crack. You can't drink at church, I told myself. Unfortunately, three weeks later I turned up to church drunk.

It was during this time that my first daughter,

Phoenix, was born. I thought that having another child would make me pull my head in, especially a little girl. There's something about men having their first daughter — they want to be their protector. I was trying to clean up my life, be a good dad and partner, and hold down an NRL career — a tough balancing act.

The penny finally dropped during a trip to Yass for a touch football game. I was talking to a close friend, Fergo, with whom I'd done a lot of partying over the years. Somehow our conversation made me admit to myself that I had a major problem with alcohol and drugs and that I had to do something about it because I was not being a decent partner or father. Not only that, I was starting to engage in some risky behaviours, such as hanging around bars until all hours of the morning, even to the point of dodging police and having run-ins with dodgy characters in Kings Cross. If I didn't do something, there was a chance I'd end up dead or serving a fair stint in prison.

The very next week I joined Alcoholics Anonymous, knowing it was essential if I was to get my footy and my life back on track.

But, despite acknowledging I had a drinking and drug problem, I didn't for one second think I might have a mental health problem. I thought that someone who was mentally unwell was 'weird' or not stable in society. I even believed that mentally ill people were criminals.

How wrong I turned out to be.

8

GETTING CLEAN

My early days with Alcoholics Anonymous (AA) and the whole journey to sobriety were extremely tough. I was still playing for Souths; I was scared that someone at AA would recognise me, and the word would get out to the press. I was so paranoid I wore a hood to meetings and pulled it down over my eyes.

The only way I could stay sober was to not let myself get anywhere near a bar or any place with alcohol. There were times when I'd lock myself in my house knowing that if I went out, the noise inside my head would direct me to a bar of some sort. I went to every effort to stay away from alcohol, so much so I even lost some friends.

Back then, there was a fairly heavy drinking culture among NRL players, so it was difficult to remain alcohol-free. The attitude of the majority of the boys was that you trained hard during the week, played hard on the weekend and then partied hard after the games. Most people I knew couldn't understand why I was giving away alcohol.

My teammates and coach knew little about the disease of alcoholism, so it was a struggle to not pick up a drink and to stay drug-free. Once I asked my coach if I could be excused from going on a cruise for a Christmas function because I was committed to staying sober and knew it would be hard to fight the temptation to drink.

'It's okay to have a few quiet drinks,' he said, 'just as long as you don't go over the top.'

It wasn't okay, not for me.

A couple of weeks later, we headed back to Wagga for Christmas. I was anxious about how I'd cope. Christmas had always been a huge party in our family — food, alcohol, music and good times. It was a Williams' tradition for Dad to put on a keg of beer and whoever turned up would bring spirits or whatever they wanted. Many relations, including Dad and myself, could play guitar and sing, so we'd pass the guitar around and sing all night, and during the days that followed.

But now I was sober, it was going to be a tough situation to come into. My sobriety was really

The only way I could stay sober was to not to let myself anywhere near a bar or any place with alcohol.

important to me, so I didn't want to drink or be around it.

I called Dad. 'I'm not coming home if there's any alcohol in the house,' I said.

Dad agreed. It was more important to have everyone together, he said.

Relieved, I loaded up the car and we drove the five hours from Sydney to Wagga. But when we arrived, I could tell that Dad had had a skin full. He was full of Christmas cheer and was well under the weather.

I turned to Suzie. 'Get the kids back in the car,' I said. 'We're going home.' I'd already gone through ten months of sobriety, and saw how my life had improved. I'd go to any lengths to keep it that way.

When Dad heard me and saw that I was serious, he stood up and asked me to stay.

'No, Dad, this is important to me,' I said. 'I told you I wouldn't come home if there was any alcohol in the house. But there is, so I'm going. We're going.'

Dad knew I was dead serious. After a few short words, he made the biggest commitment to me to date. 'Joe,' he said. 'I'm sorry, I broke my word. I'll get sober tomorrow. Will you take me to one of your meetings?'

Since then, there have been many different situations during which Dad could have picked up a drink but didn't. We are now both twelve years sober — together.

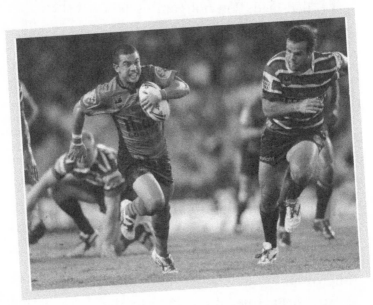

Always run faster when you are being chased
— especially by bigger guys.

Later in 2007, I played the majority of games in the top grade, but I also played a string of games with the reserve-grade team, the North Sydney Bears, which was the feeder club for the Rabbitohs. We had an awesome team and got through the finals series to qualify for the grand final, which we were raging favourites to win.

Despite it being a reserve-grade team, thirteen of the seventeen-man North Sydney Bears squad had played first grade, either during the 2007 season or before. The grand final also had special significance as it was going to be the last game for my childhood hero, David Peachey.

All week I was excited, but I was dreading the post-game events. Win or lose, traditionally, footy teams go out on the night they finish the season and continue to party through to 'Mad Monday'. The whispers in my head were convincing me that it wasn't every day you won a grand final. Surely I could have a few quiet beers if we won, they said, even though I knew that these types of celebrations were never quiet and that limiting myself to a couple of beers would be a massive challenge.

The game turned out to be a fairly dour affair, with our team far from its best. There was a horrendous wind that played havoc for the goal kickers. I'd had a roughly 75 to 80 per cent success rate during the year, but on that day I only managed one conversion from seven attempts.

Despite my disastrous day with the boot, the score was level with just a little over two minutes remaining on the clock. We had the ball and were making our way up the field with the plan that, as soon as we were close enough, I'd attempt a field goal. We managed to get within goal-scoring range, and the ball came to me — and while it wasn't the prettiest of kicks coming off the boot, it managed to scrape over the crossbar.

I did it again, I thought to myself, just as I had done in the Under 20s grand final five years earlier. I was already picturing the after-game party in my mind. All we had to do was hold Parramatta, the opposing team, out for one minute.

Well, that day, Parramatta had other plans. I'm not quite sure how they got the ball back from the kick-off, but they quickly had us under pressure. We were desperately defending our line when, just as the siren sounded, the Parramatta backrower, Weller Hauraki, crashed over beside the post and slammed the ball down for a winning try.

I was shattered, and the team was shattered. We'd lost the grand final. We'd so wanted to send our brother Peach off with a career-ending win, and we'd tried so hard, despite it being our worst game of the season.

Looking back to that grand final, there is one thing I'm thankful for, though it's a little selfish. But because we lost I got to stay sober.

Dave Peachey (centre left) after North Sydney's loss to Paramatta in the 2007 reserve-grade grand final. That's me crouching on the right.

I distinctly remember saying to myself when I saw Weller crash over, 'You didn't win, so there's no excuse now to get on the drink over the next couple of days. Losers don't celebrate.'

I managed to keep myself away from the team after the game and through the grand final evening, going to the leagues club with family members aware of my struggle with alcohol and drugs. We only stayed there for an hour or so; I had a couple of soft drinks and was home before 11pm.

When 'Mad Monday' came around, I turned my phone off so I wouldn't receive any calls from my teammates. And when Suzie and our kids, Brodi and Phoenix, had to go somewhere that day, I asked her to deadlock the doors and take the keys so I couldn't get out of the house. However, as soon as Suzie and the kids left, I was overcome by an immediate urge to get hold of as much alcohol as I could lay my hands on. It was during those hours while my family was gone from the house that I experienced my worst-ever alcohol and drug cravings. I remember walking around the house to the point of almost pulling my hair out, saying to myself, 'If I can make it through this tough time, I can make it through anything.' And I made a vow to myself that if I got through it I would get the Serenity Prayer tattooed onto my torso.

The AA motto is to live one day at a time, but in order to get through that day I had to break the time down into tiny pieces, from every hour into every minute. At times I even found myself staring at a clock on the wall while I counted the seconds.

Having survived that Monday, I felt I could get through the toughest of tests. The following day I got the Serenity Prayer tattooed onto my torso, as a reminder that if I could get through that day, I can get through any day.

9

TURNING TO PRESCRIPTION DRUGS

I was clean and sober for over a year, but fighting my addictions to party drugs and alcohol was a major battle. I was haunted by the constant barrage of negative conversations in my head, which took a heavy toll. Drinking alcohol and taking drugs quietened down the noise. Giving them away turned the noise back up — right up! It was during this time I experienced my first serious bout of depression.

I was doing my best to hold my position in an NRL team, and I couldn't understand why I was down all the time. I began looking for something to fill the void, and unfortunately I turned to prescription drugs. These gave me a feeling of being out of it or 'high' in a similar way to illicit drugs. As well, they weren't detected by drug tests.

It was easy to access prescription drugs by lying to doctors or getting prescriptions from injured players. Soon my addiction to the prescription drug high was so strong I couldn't wait to go home after training and get completely out of it by taking extreme amounts of sleeping pills, painkillers and antipsychotic pills. You name it, I had a crack at it.

Eventually, I realised I was hooked. The only difference was that taking prescription drugs wouldn't land me in prison. During the worst times, when the voices in my head were really loud, I'd take as many pills as I could, testing my tolerance and even chancing the thought I wouldn't wake up. It was like I was addicted to the thrill — I was walking the fine line between life and death, and I was loving it.

Of course, my behaviour was putting a strain on my relationship at home. There were days when I would come home from training, my kids would be jumping all over me, wanting to play, and I was too high to even register they were there.

It got to the point that the voices in my head were telling me constantly I was no longer worthy to be alive, and the world would be a better place without me. The louder and more constant the voices became, the more drugs I took. The only way that I could deal with the negative voices telling me to kill myself was to get completely shit-faced.

I began taking prescription pills at any time of the day. Then, at the end of the 2007 season, I left

The head noise was out of control again, and I was using prescription drugs to silence it.

Souths and signed with Penrith. But after we were beaten by the Brisbane Broncos in the first game, I was dropped to reserve grade.

In all honesty, this was when I began to lose interest in the game I'd loved for so long. The head noise was out of control again, and I was using prescription drugs to silence it.

Once, when I was playing in Penrith's reserve-grade team, we were travelling to New Zealand for a game. I felt so low on the flight to Auckland I took a full tray of prescription sleeping pills, not caring whether or not I woke up. The only thing I remember from that trip was my roommate saying: 'Joey, this isn't good, man. You really shouldn't take that many pills.' But I didn't care. It was like his words went in one ear and out the other. And when I was taking pills, I also didn't care if we won or lost, or whether I played well or badly.

Finally I realised that, yet again, I was addicted and would have to try to break my addiction. Fearing I'd be banished from the NRL if I tried to get professional help and was found out, I decided to go cold turkey.

That detox was one of the worst experiences I've ever had. During the height of my prescription pill addiction, I hadn't been able to fall asleep by myself without the aid of far too many pills. I was so used to using pills to get to sleep, I barely got any sleep at all during the first 36 hours of detoxing. Then there were the hot and cold sweats and hallucinations. I got so paranoid at one point, I was afraid to leave my bedroom and believed the world was against me. When I wasn't at football training, I'd stay at home, doors locked and the blinds closed.

Once more I'd hit rock bottom, but somehow I'd again crawled out of the hole. Now, somehow, I needed to stay clean and get my life together.

10

FINDING MY LIFELINE

Midway through the 2008 season, I walked into the Redfern PCYC to see champion boxing trainer Johnny Lewis. Johnny and I had run into each other a year or so earlier, and he'd mentioned his connection to Cowra and how he'd met my dad when he was playing football in Sydney. 'Give me a buzz,' he'd said, 'if you ever need any extra fitness work.'

Around the same time, bitter that I was still playing reserve-grade, I asked my manager to look for an opportunity for me to get back in the top grade, maybe with another club. I was kicking stones and not enjoying playing footy at all, but, looking back, I would have been better off if I'd ripped in at training to get back into first grade. Hindsight ...

Eventually, I got a release and signed on to play

with the Canterbury Bulldogs. But I'd learned in AA that the one thing you take with you everywhere is yourself. So even though I'd moved clubs, my problems were still with me. Now, I'd also lost all interest in the game. Playing in the NRL felt like just a job. So, at the end of that 2008 season, I walked away from rugby league.

This time, when I met with Johnny at Redfern PCYC, I wasn't looking to get back on the rugby league field. Instead, I wanted to see if I could make it as a boxer. And that's what we did.

Johnny Lewis — a great man whom
I love and respect dearly.

I hadn't been the most aggressive rugby league player, and my form had always been up and down, particularly during the worst of my addiction problems. As a result, a lot of people didn't think I could make it as a boxer. And for sure, boxing training is much harder than playing league. But in addition to improving my physical fitness, boxing gave me something I had never gotten from the game. Boxing increased my mental toughness.

In the weeks that followed, I also realised that the harder I worked in the boxing gym, the quieter the noise in my head. In working my physical fitness, I began to build a resilience to the negative talk that was happening between my ears.

When I walked into that boxing gym, I felt like a weight had been lifted from my shoulders, and my demons and mental health battles were diminished. During the time I spent inside those four walls my mind was free, and I came to love the discipline and hard work involved.

Johnny had a lot to do with it. He's the best motivator I've ever known. He has a calming effect that makes you feel safe. Even when my heart was beating through my chest and anxiety was causing my thoughts to spiral out of control, Johnny's soft whispers of 'C'mon, Joey, pick up the pace a bit, son,' would calm me. And even when I was hitting the pads, not an ounce of energy left in my body, Johnny's words could convince me to find that little bit more.

Dad would say: 'Joe, if you think you're fit enough to box, keep training harder.' Boxing taught me

When I walked into that boxing gym I felt like a weight had been lifted from my shoulders.

discipline and to work right to the final bell of each round.

Soon I found I was applying the same discipline beyond the gym. I was getting up every morning at 6 am to run, and keeping to a strict diet, because I had to get my weight down from a footy player's 82 kilos to the weight I eventually fought my first fight at — 69 kilos.

Eventually, after I'd been training tirelessly with Johnny for a few months, he said to me: 'Do you want a fight?'

I didn't know what to say — training was very different to the real thing — but I thought, why not?

Usually in boxing, you fight as an amateur, then, if you go okay, you move into the professional ranks. Johnny thought I would be all right moving straight

Boxing taught me discipline, and to work right to the final bell of each round.

to the pros. So I began to get ready for my first professional boxing fight.

On the night of my first fight, at Punchbowl Croatian Club, I was the most nervous I've ever been in my life. I began to question everything about my preparation: had I done enough?

Luckily, I had Johnny Lewis in my corner, a man who always has a calm head. Johnny doesn't say much, but when he does, you listen.

I ended up winning my first fight with a second-round knockout. And under Johnny's coaching, I went on to win the next two fights. Thanks to boxing, and Johnny Lewis, I felt like I might be getting my life back on track.

11

LOSING MY GRIP

Living in Sydney is expensive, so Suzie, Brodi, Phoenix and I moved back to Wagga. I'd never been a big fan of city life, despite living there for many years, and it was great to have family around to help with the kids.

Back home in Wagga, I teamed up with Dad and a great man in the boxing circles, Jeff Malcolm. Dad had known Jeff from his time playing football in Sydney with Wests Magpies. Jeff was a world-rated boxer and had also been trained by Johnny Lewis, so it was a great fit.

But in early 2010, my marriage to Suzie broke down. It was destructive and very painful for both of us. For fifteen months after our separation, I didn't get to see or speak to Brodi or Phoenix, which sent my mood even lower. Going from living and interacting with my children every single day to not seeing or speaking to them for over a year took a heavy toll. It got to the point where, some days, I couldn't physically get out of bed. I'd lose hours in the day, passing time by self-medicating with prescription drugs. But, I didn't pick up a drink or a party drug. This was a step in the right direction.

The fifteen months apart from my kids took a heavy toll on my relationship with them. I don't blame them — I believe Brodi and Phoenix truly do love me, but without doubt they are closer to

I'd lose hours in the day, passing time by self-medicating with prescription drugs.

their mother. I can only try to continue to build on the relationship we have, by showing them I love them every day.

Finally, I decided to seek professional help for my low mood, because surviving from day to day had become too hard. That's when I was diagnosed with bipolar disorder and learned that it caused my mood to swing from terrible lows to manic highs (mania).

At last I understood why there were times when I felt infallible. During those manic highs, I might go on spending sprees, when I'd be going through a great deal of money, sometimes resorting to borrowing to keep the spending spree going.

When I was first diagnosed with bipolar disorder, I didn't know anything about the illness, but I'd heard all kinds of things, many of them wrong. As time passed, though, I did some research and eventually met other people with the same thing. The more people I met with bipolar, the more similarities I would recognise, and the more I realised I wasn't alone and I wasn't so unusual after all. But it was daunting to be diagnosed with a mental illness, and there was still a stigma around it, so it wasn't a tag I wore proudly.

I was still boxing and had continued undefeated. Then an offer came through to play rugby league for a French team, Sporting Olympique Avignon XIII, based in Avignon, a beautiful city in the south of France. Rugby league wasn't a huge game in France back then, and the competition was still very much in development. But the money was good, so I decided to play a season there and see whether I liked it. I'd started a relationship with a girl from Dubbo named Tegan, so we agreed to move to France together.

It was quite tough playing halfback in a team where only a few people understood English. As a halfback, your job is to push the team around the park and be the number-one communicator, telling everyone where to go. On the field, things were going okay. We won a few games, and when you're winning in France, you're treated like royalty. When you're losing, not so much.

Off the field, though, things weren't so great. Both of us were homesick, and I was missing my kids terribly. We were excited when Tegan fell pregnant, and decided to move back to Australia, to Tegan's home town of Dubbo. I'd keep playing footy, this time with country rugby league powerhouse Dubbo CYMS.

I had great times playing with CYMS. We won the premiership, and the following season I captain-coached and we were runners-up.

During our first year in Dubbo, our son Rome was born. But not long after, Tegan and I separated. It was a rough time. There was name-calling, anger and bitterness, which took their toll, not only physically, but mentally. For my entire life, all I wanted to be was a good dad. And now I had three children from two relationships, but I wasn't living with any of them.

After hearing you're a worthless, good-for-nothing, terrible father from not just one but two different mothers of your kids, you start to believe

Finally I decided to seek professional help for my low mood.

it. And for the most part they were correct. I wasn't being the best father, but I think a lot of that was because I was severely mentally unwell.

It was during this time I stopped taking my medication for my bipolar disorder for six months, thinking I could get by without it. I was wrong — I went through a very tough mental battle with the negative voices returning, telling me I didn't deserve to be alive, the world would be better off without me, I was a burden to my kids. I was in such a dark space that I started to believe the voices. No matter what I did or how much I tried to get my mind away from that space, the only thing I could think of was that I just wanted it all to go away.

I began to think killing myself was the only way to make the pain go away. I also began to believe my three children — Brodi, Phoenix and Rome — would be better off without me in their life, that my family didn't love me and I was a burden to everyone.

I was in such a dark space that I started to believe the voices.

I remember the day I decided to end my life as if it were yesterday. The noise inside my head was so loud I couldn't think of anything else but to make it all disappear. And it felt like the only way to do this was to end my life. The voices and screams to end my life became so loud and vivid in my head it was terrifying. At one stage, I lay on the floor of the shower in the foetal position, shaking and rocking back and forth, fighting with the voices screaming at me to kill myself.

In that critical moment, I made up my mind that the only way to make the shrieking in my head disappear was to end my life. Many people have asked, did I think about my family or my kids? I can honestly say that my kids mean the absolute world to me but, on that day, in that dire moment, I couldn't think of anything else but making the noise stop by ending my life. So no, I did not think of my kids. That doesn't mean that I didn't love them; it just means I was in horrendous mental pain and the only way I could make it all go away was to not be on this earth any longer.

In all my years of playing rugby league and being in fights in and out of the boxing ring, I had never been as scared as I was right then. I didn't want to die, I just wanted the mental pain to stop, and the only way I believed it would stop was to end my life.

Eventually I dragged myself out of the shower and wrote letters to each of my kids, apologising that I wouldn't be around to be their dad, apologising that

I didn't want to die, I just wanted the mental pain to stop.

I wouldn't get to see my daughter Phoenix walk down the aisle or watch the boys play footy, and that I wouldn't be around to see them graduate from school. I told them that I'd never ever be far and if they ever needed me to just look up. I placed the letters directly next to my phone beside my bed, but I couldn't pick up the phone to make a call for help.

In that moment, I didn't want help — I wanted the pain to end.

After I'd finished writing letters to my kids, I swallowed as many sleeping pills, antidepressants, antipsychotics and other pills as I could find in my house. I was content that the world, my kids and everyone else would be better off without me in their life. I lay down on the bed and slowly began to drift off. I hoped I would never wake up.

12

ALIVE

The following day I woke, extremely dazed and confused — but alive. I didn't know whether to be angry that I hadn't succeeded in killing myself, or thankful that I'd survived. *I just tried to end my life*, I thought to myself, *but something much more powerful than me has kept me here. I've been given a second chance.*

As it turned out, while I was in a completely out-of-it state I'd rung and told one of my closest friends, Leigh Burns, about what I'd done. Leigh and I had grown up together in Cowra, and even though we were heading in different directions in our lives, we'd always remained extremely close. I often called Leigh to talk my problems out. After she spoke to me that night, Leigh called a family member, and that family member told my dad, who happened to be in Cowra.

Dad found out the following morning, and rang me straight away, concerned. He didn't want to believe it was true until he heard the words come from my mouth.

'Yes, Dad, last night I tried to kill myself.'

Without hesitation, Dad drove straight to Dubbo. Leigh was worried I'd be upset with her that my parents had found out, but in all honesty it was a relief. I could finally talk to my family about how suicidal I'd been feeling. I didn't have to carry that burden alone any longer. It's a tough situation – you want to be able to speak to someone, but you're afraid they'll judge you so you keep it all in.

After Dad told Mum what had happened, she rang me in tears. She told me she loved me and that I needed to talk to someone when I was feeling low. I tried to explain to her that, while I knew the right thing to do was talk to another person, for many reasons it was the last thing I'd wanted to do. I didn't want to be a burden. I thought people wouldn't understand what I was going through.

Spending the weekend with my father was great and I was feeling a bit better by the time he left, but a week later, things hadn't improved, and I realised that the illness was too strong for me, I couldn't deal with it alone any longer. I needed professional help. In hindsight, it would have been better for my dad to take me straight to the hospital, but this was a first for anyone in our family.

It was Tegan who took me to the hospital for a mental health assessment. After I told the doctor about the way I'd been feeling, the constant voices

A week later, things hadn't improved, and I realised that the illness was too strong for me.

in my head and the type and number of drugs I had taken in my suicide attempt, he said I was extremely lucky to be alive. For my own safety he said I needed to be admitted to the local mental health ward.

Hearing those words come out of a doctor's mouth made me feel a great deal of shame and guilt, but I knew deep down that the best thing for me to do was to follow his advice. I agreed to be admitted and spent the next three nights in the mental health ward.

On the first day I was heavily sedated, but I was thankful to be in a place where I was able to get help, remain completely anonymous and not be judged. I'd always felt there was a stigma about mental illness, so I'd never been in a rush to make my battles public, for fear of being ridiculed or made fun of. This was the most vulnerable I'd ever felt, so it was an extremely scary time.

I was forced to do an inventory of myself: how I was feeling and what I'd been going through and doing in the weeks leading up to my suicide attempt. And with support, I also did some soul searching. I came to the realisation that I'd been given a second chance at life. After I was better, I decided, I would help other people suffering from similar issues.

The idea was sparked when a lady who was in the psych unit for similar reasons approached me. 'Joe Williams,' she said, 'whoever would have thought you were like us?'

At first I was embarrassed, but her words got me thinking. As a prominent sportsperson living with bipolar disorder, I could help other people suffering from a mental illness with their recovery. But in order to do that, I had to start managing my own life. That was the challenge.

———

One afternoon not long after I'd been released from the Dubbo psych unit, Dad and I were sitting on the front step of my home. 'I want to tell you the story of the little boy inside us all,' he said. 'There's a little boy (or girl) who lives in us all. He's either guided by you, or he controls you. Every now and then, that little boy encounters a situation that frightens him to the point that he wants to go deep inside and hide, to not show his face. In each situation, he's faced with a door that he can either walk through, or go back and hide from. You're with this little boy. You come to the door — what do you do?'

'Kick the door down so he can walk through,' I quickly replied.

My father's reply implanted a seed in my mind that has since helped me conquer my inner fears. 'Take that little boy by the hand,' he said, 'and say to him, "I'm here with you. Let's do this together." Lead that little boy, be his guiding light, together as one. Together you can conquer any obstacle you face.'

I still carry this advice with me. I still have fears and insecurities in my life, just like everyone, when the little boy in here wants to hide — but now I know to guide him through rather than let him control me.

During those days, Dad and I would sit and talk for hours. There was laughter, pain and many tears. At one point he told me how he and his brothers and sisters had felt, growing up without a father. For me, that was the moment we finally bonded as men.

———

It was in Dubbo that I met a girl called Courtney Merritt. I still didn't know many people in the town, but I knew Courtney's cousin Morgan through Tegan, and through Morgan I met Courtney.

Courtney was, and to some degree still is, an extremely shy person, so when I saw her around town after we met I'd say hello, but we never had any real conversations and there were lots of awkward silences. But over time, Courtney and I started hanging out a lot more, though I always had to initiate any conversations between us.

After knowing her for a while, we organised for her to come over to my place to watch a movie and hang out. On the night she was supposed to come over it was raining heavily, and she was absolutely drenched when she arrived. I asked how she got so wet, because even though it was raining she looked like she'd been standing in a shower. She told me she'd been too embarrassed to tell her grandmother she was going to a boy's house, so she'd got her nan to

After I was better, I decided, I wanted to help other people suffering from similar issues.

drop her around the corner from my house. Little did she realise that her nan would wait to see if she got in the house okay — awkward when you're standing in the rain, outside a house belonging to people you don't know. After waiting for several minutes, her nan finally drove off, and Courtney walked around the corner in the pouring rain to my house.

I didn't know a great deal about Courtney in the beginning, but as we became closer and she started opening up about her journey, I realised that she was quite the caring soul. But despite how much I liked her, I didn't want to scare her away by telling her about my suicide attempt because of all the stigma surrounding mental illness and suicide.

It was after Courtney told me more about her childhood and upbringing that I got an appreciation for the toughness that isn't obvious in this shy, quiet woman. When she was three years old, she'd been diagnosed with leukaemia. She was treated with chemotherapy and radiotherapy, but the doctors gave her very little chance of survival.

Despite this, three-year-old Courtney fought on and began to slowly get better. In a terrible twist of fate, as Courtney started to improve, her mother, Ann Maree, was diagnosed with leukaemia and she passed away.

The first time Courtney told me this story, tears welled in her eyes but she never cried. It was after hearing Courtney's story that I decided to tell her more about my past, including my suicide attempt. From top to bottom, she was inquisitive and genuinely caring, which made me realise she was different. Courtney was someone I could trust, someone I could lean on when times got tough. And she could do the same with me. It made all the difference. With Courtney by my side, I had a chance of taking charge of my own life, and helping other people do the same.

13

BACK INTO BOXING

It was during my stay in the Dubbo psych unit that Mum found out she had a large aneurysm on her brain. The day she got the results, the doctor told her she should go straight to Sydney the next day for further tests. Knowing Dad would be an emotional mess in Sydney, I decided to drive to Sydney the next morning without telling them, so I could be there. As soon as the elevator doors opened and Dad saw me, tears trickled down his face. Not usually one to show his emotions, it was clear he was thankful to have the support.

The scans in Sydney revealed that Mum had not one but nine separate brain aneurysms. In the end, Mum had to have two separate brain surgeries, and she spent over five weeks in intensive care. It was a massive scare for the whole family, as Mum is our rock and we didn't know whether she'd make it through and make a full recovery.

Of course, with time, and true to Mum's character, she did. Apart from some memory problems at times, she's back to her best, giving orders and caring for us all. People say and think the boys in our family are the tough ones, but without a doubt, Mum has just as much credibility in that corner.

The Bosses — Mum and Dad.

Courtney and I decided to move back to Wagga. Since my suicide attempt, Dubbo had had a negative vibe for me, and I needed to get away. A huge part of returning home to Wagga was to be closer to family, especially Mum, who was still recovering from her surgery.

There I was lucky enough to score a job working at a local Catholic high school as the Aboriginal Education Worker, helping to look after students' welfare and helping out with their school work. At the same time, my relationship with Dad continued to build. Dad became my boxing coach, and we spent hours together in the gym. He'd also ride a bike alongside me when I was road running, and we spent long stretches of time together in the car, preparing my fight plan and going over any mistakes I'd made in the gym.

I'd also travel to Sydney to train under world-class boxing coach Billy Hussein, someone I now greatly admire and consider a brother. Billy has had huge success as a coach, and I believe the reason is not only due to his boxers' talent, work ethic and ability but also to the attitude towards life he instils in them outside the boxing ring. Billy talked about how he sets his fighters up mentally for a lifestyle they can be proud of — a life of humility, poise and value. Billy provides his fighters with a culture to be better people. It was just what I needed at that time in my life, and it has stayed with me ever since.

For example, something that struck me the first few times I trained under Billy was that whenever his boxers came into the gym, they walked around to every single person, shook hands and asked them how they were doing. Now, that might not seem like much, but to me it spoke of the value and humility of every fighter that Billy Hussein trained. Billy didn't just train us to be boxers, he trained us to be humble young men. There were rules in Billy's gym, no matter who you were or where you sat, and everyone followed the values, not just because they were the rules but because they were good values to have in life.

In 2013, I started training for my first-ever World Boxing Foundation (WBF) world title fight, against Brett William Smith. The fight was for the lightweight title — 61.2 kilograms. I'd never fought at that weight before — previously I'd been fighting at the division above, Junior Welterweight, which was 63.5 kilograms. But I wasn't going to back away from the fight because I couldn't make the weight.

Billy Hussein — I learnt so much from this man, more than boxing, about creating your own positive life culture.

I worked incredibly hard to get my weight down. But when I got to Brisbane for the weigh-in, I was still 2 kilos above the weight limit. I'd already stopped drinking water and consuming food thirty-six hours earlier, to get my weight down as much as possible. Now I sat in a hot bath with Epsom salts, to drain the water out of my body.

I spent the entire day in and out of the sauna — in for ten minutes, out for ten minutes. After every ten minutes, I'd check my weight on some scales they had at the gym. Slowly it came down. I'll never forget the mental toughness I had to draw on that day.

It was a huge relief when I finally made weight. By the time I got to the weigh-in, I had no energy

Billy didn't just train us to be boxers, he trained us to be humble young men.

but was stoked to be able to have a meal and some water once it was done.

But when I got to the weigh-in, the scales said I was 61.8 kilograms — over the limit by 600 grams. It doesn't sound like much, but given I hadn't eaten for two days or had a drink of water, I had no idea how I'd be able to lose the extra weight in time.

I was struggling mentally and physically. But in boxing, you can't show any vulnerability. I had to get the weight off, and I had only two hours to do it.

So we headed for the closest sauna. Inside the sauna, I started running back and forth, trying to make my body sweat (sweat equals fluid, which equals weight). I finally made weight.

With a short time to spare, we rushed back to the weigh-in venue and weighed in. I'd done it — I'd made weight. With a sigh of relief and a hug from Dad, I could relax a little and refuel with as much food and fluid as possible.

Then it was fight time. Unfortunately, the fight didn't go to plan. I was completely zapped and had no power. The gruelling weight cut had proved too much. Not that I'm taking anything away from Brett William Smith, my opponent. He did everything he needed to get me out of there that night, and I was eventually sent to the canvas with a beautifully timed right hand to the temple.

After the fight, people asked whether I was disappointed. Of course I was, no-one likes to lose — but I found comfort in the fact that I'd been to a place I had never been before with the

I was alive to tell the tale, and had just fought for a WBF title. Things could be a lot worse ...

weight challenge. I could also feel proud that, less than twelve months prior, I'd tried to take my life by suicide. I was alive to tell the tale, and had just fought for a WBF title. Things could be a lot worse ...

In the end, I had two more shots at the WBF title in the junior welterweight division that I'd fought in for most of my career, and I won those fights. When I finally retired, I was two time WBF Junior Welterweight Champion, and WBC Asia Continental Champion. I ended up with twelve wins from sixteen fights, but it's not the numbers that count, in my eyes, because boxing taught me how to win at life.

Top: When in doubt, stick the jab out.
Bottom: After my last win against Kie Raha — belt collecting.

14

MAKING A DIFFERENCE

I'd been doing my boxing training out of Mum and Dad's back shed in Wagga, or sometimes, on the odd occasion, at the Wagga PCYC. Neither was perfect — sometimes the PCYC would be closed, and Mum and Dad's shed had the barest of essentials. I was also helping to train my friend, Dave Letele, who was having some issues with his weigh. Dave was running a supermarket not far from Wagga and would travel across twice a week to train with me.

Dave's supermarket was a private sponsor of mine to help with my boxing, and one day we got into a conversation about starting a gym, a place where not only I could train but I could also train others. So that's what we did. A year or so later, Joe Williams Boxing

(JWB) Gym was born. The gym attracted everyone from school-aged kids to people over the age of fifty, and it helped many get their fitness journey on track. It was also a fantastic place for conversation, smiles, laughter and, of course, hard work.

I loved the sense of community at the gym, and it inspired me to get involved with more community fundraising. One charity I still hold dear to my heart is the Amie St Clair Melanoma Trust. I'd grown up next door to Pete and Annette St Clair and their kids Amie and Tim. But just a day after her twenty-first birthday, Amie, a loving, caring, outgoing girl who lived life to the full, tragically lost her life due to melanoma. These days, as a result, I always jump at any opportunity to raise funds and awareness around melanoma and skin cancer.

I also became involved in Wagga Wagga Takes 2, a singing competition that pairs up local Wagga singers with each other or with people of note within the community. Having grown up with music and always loved the feeling of being on stage in front of a band, I jumped at the opportunity to perform on Wagga Wagga Takes 2. Each singer chose a local charity to support. The competition was not only about singing but also about raising money for charity.

When I first participated in Wagga Wagga Takes 2 in 2013 with Shelley McCormack, one of the other contestants had already chosen the Amie St Clair Melanoma Trust as their charity, so I opted for The Cancer Council — Wagga Relay for Life. Raising money for a cancer charity was important to me because I had lost many family and friends to cancer.

Each contestant had to organise a fundraiser for their local charity. As I was running my own boxing and cardio-fitness gym, I decided to do something outside the square and host a twenty-four hours charity treadmill run. This involved setting up two treadmills, and having someone running on at least one treadmill for the entire twenty-four hours. The idea was to make it a community event, breaking the twenty-four hours down to fifteen-minute timeslots and filling as many timeslots as I could with people from the Wagga community.

I put the call out for people to participate. The response was great, with Wagga people showing true community spirit. We had volunteers ranging from family and friends to students from the school I was working at, ladies aged sixty-plus, local sporting identities and entire families of mothers, fathers and kids. This was typical of Wagga — everyone jumped behind a local charity event to raise funds.

The Cancer Council staff put on a barbecue, as well as tea and coffee for the entire twenty-four hours. As well as committing time, various local sponsors donated treadmills, clothing and water. People had the choice to donate online, come in and donate cash, or purchase raffle tickets. There was also a twenty-four hour live auction for an Aboriginal hand-painted AFL Sydney Swans jersey signed by Australian of the Year Adam Goodes.

Me and Court at the Amie St Clair Melanoma Ball. I need heels!

I was the first cab off the rank on the treadmills. But even when I wasn't on the treadmill, I had to stick around to make sure everything ran smoothly. As it turned out, all the runners turned up on time and people dropped by to cheer on friends and

We had volunteers ranging from family and friends to students from the school I was working at.

make a donation. We had all types of people come in, from larrikins who'd been at the local drinking hole to police officers. Some girls even randomly popped in and 'touched up' their make-up while they waited for a couple of the local footy studs to hit the treadmill. Other girls paid extra money to see the boys run with no shirt on (all for charity, they said).

We made it through the night with no major hiccups. As the afternoon approached, we were getting down to the final runners. I chose to start and finish the event and ended up doing seven hours in total on the treadmill. As I completed the final hour, my family were there to count me down to the finish.

In the end, with all the money we counted from raffles, the auction and donations, we raised over $10,000. It was an awesome achievement by everyone and a great way to get the fundraising up and running.

For me, it was the start of something that has made me stronger and taught me to be grateful for what I have and to feel compassion for others. Moving forward, I was finding that focusing on gratefulness and compassion helped keep my erratic moods under control.

15

MENTORS: WE ALL NEED THEM

Working at the gym also gave me a chance to help out other people. One such person was a friend of mine, Steve 'Slip' Morris. Like me, Slip was born in Wiradjuri country, but his mother came from the Barkindji Nation around Wilcannia.

I'd first heard his name mentioned when I was with Tegan, Rome's mother. She'd mentioned how this guy, Steve, had been messaging her. From that point, without even knowing who he was, I didn't trust him. Later, I heard he was a talented footballer and had played short stints of league in Sydney but had always come home to the country. I also heard he lived in Forbes, liked a party, and was a bit of a ladies' man.

I was playing a music gig in Parkes in New South Wales one night, when someone pointed out Steve. I looked over and saw him walking around the venue like he owned the place. Then I ran into him at the bar. We looked each other up and down, said hello then drifted off.

Later that evening, a mutual friend introduced us. We got to talking about life, footy and other stuff, and ended up getting on well, losing the egotistical edge of two bulls arguing over who ruled the paddock.

A week or so later, I received a message from Steve saying he was in Wagga and would love to catch up at the footy. We had a great time when we met up, and I introduced him to my dad. Steve mentioned he was moving to Wagga to play footy.

After he arrived in town, he told me he wanted to start boxing to improve his fitness. I knew that, in Forbes, he'd gone from a kid who had enormous potential to play in the NRL, to someone who drank in a bar till closing time, then bought a carton of beer to take home to drink by himself. The next day he'd wake up, go to work and do it all over again.

Without Steve saying anything to me, I could see he was reaching out to better his life. He was sick of living the party lifestyle, and saw limited purpose

Steve 'Slip' Morris and me.

in what he was doing. I knew from my own experience that boxing had the potential to improve your physical, mental and emotional health, and make it easier to get through tough times. So my plan was for Slip to do some boxing cardio work to help him shed a few kilograms. But mostly I wanted to just have him hang around positive people like

Dad and myself, people who didn't drink alcohol or take drugs, rather than people who had a negative impact on him. I reasoned that with Steve hanging out and training with us at JWB, any negative friends would tend to stay away.

We got started, and a day at a time, week after week, Steve kept coming back. As I got to know him better, I realised how very similar we were in our thinking and our sense of humour. In fact, we became such good friends that Courtney and I ended up moving in with Steve and his partner at the time, only moving out just before our first child together, Ari, was born.

After a while, Steve started running some of my classes for me while I was preparing for upcoming fights, allowing me the time and space to prepare and concentrate on the task at hand.

So from starting off as enemies, Steve and I had moved on to becoming mates then unofficial mentor and mentee at JWB to living together. Soon Steve became a member of the JWB team and ended up helping prepare me for fights as well as helping with the logistics on the night.

Before we knew it, he was approaching twelve months completely free of all alcohol and drugs —

all by hanging out with good people and adopting a positive lifestyle.

But life throws us curve balls from all directions. Steve went through a tough patch in his relationship and was travelling in a pretty dark place. Knowing his background, I had a gut feeling that something wasn't right. I tried to ring him about five times, but all my calls went straight through to message bank. So I drove around to his apartment. I walked into his house and, to my shock and dismay, he was curled up on the lounge-room floor, covered in his own vomit, a couple of bottles of pills nearby.

A vivid flashback of my own suicide attempt went through my mind. As I checked his pulse, he mumbled something. Knowing he was alive, I rang the emergency department of the local hospital to tell them what had happened, and then headed to the hospital with him.

When we arrived, Steve was admitted into the emergency ward and started getting the right treatment. Knowing from my own experience that the next few days would be crucial to his recovery, I did everything I could think of to help. I knew he'd feel vulnerable and confused about what had gone on during the time prior to his suicide attempt, so I wanted to make sure he had as little as possible to think about so he could concentrate on getting well.

Steve had many ups and downs during that initial hospital stay, but since then all in all he has maintained a stable life, and I couldn't be more prouder of the guy I now call my best mate.

Eventually he moved away from Wagga, and not long after he was faced with a new challenge when

I knew from my own experience that boxing had the potential to improve your physical, mental and emotional health, and make it easier to get through tough times.

he was diagnosed with lymphoma. Steve fought tooth and nail to beat it, undergoing several rounds of chemotherapy and then radiotherapy.

One day we were in the car together when Steve said to me: 'I'll beat this, brother. I won't let it win.' It was the advice I used to give him at the gym, when we both trained to the point of exhaustion. Later that afternoon, our favourite song — 'Whiskey Lullaby' by Brad Paisley — came on. I drove away in tears, not knowing if I would see my best friend again.

Several months later, Steve received the news he'd been hoping for — his blood tests had come back clear and he'd beaten his lymphoma.

Steve now lives with his fiancée and two beautiful daughters on the Central Coast of New South Wales, where he operates a mental health recovery and mentoring program. He's received numerous letters from young people he's worked with and mentored, saying how they want to be just like him when they're older. As well as this great achievement, Steve and two other Indigenous men run a recovery program called Brothers 4 Recovery (B4R). They travel across New South Wales, trying to tackle the country's drug and alcohol epidemic.

My journey with Steve had started with dislike, based on the reputation of a guy I knew nothing about. Over the years, through sweat, blood and tears, it grew into a brotherhood, and I'd like to think I played a part in his journey to recovery. Now Steve is a mate who has been my shoulder to cry on during many tough times through my mental health journey. He's also the godfather of my youngest son, Ari. Good things can happen. Sometimes you just have to work at it.

16

THE ENEMY WITHIN

Through my community work in Wagga, I got to know a business owner called Simone Dowding. Simone owns a coffee-roasting business and a string of cafes called The Blessed Bean, but she's also studied Buddhism and is a trained psychologist. Simone was seriously concerned about the suffering caused by depression and mental illness in our area. We got talking and then, one day, Simone came to me with the idea of making a documentary about my journey — my battles with mental illness and suicide ideation, and how I'd survived and thrived. The film was scripted by Simone in consultation with various psychologists, and we teamed up with an outfit called

Mayfly Media, who volunteered their time and equipment to manage the production of the film.

The aim of *The Enemy Within* was to help others suffering from mental health problems. The vision was raw, the message was beautiful.

When the film was shown as part of the Wagga Wagga Short Film Festival, I was just three days out from my WBF Junior Welterweight title defence. I hadn't previously talked publicly about my depression or suicide attempt, and now here I was, baring my soul to the community, telling everyone about my struggles with my mental health and how I tried to take my own life. Watching the film with a huge crowd of people reduced me to tears.

When it was over, I could hear the murmurs around the room. Here's Joe Williams, professional sportsperson for several years, who's struggled with depression most of his life, telling it how it is. Finally, the monkey was off my back.

While the idea behind *The Enemy Within* had been to help others come through to the other side like I had done, it helped me, too. Having my past struggles brought up again really drove home how lucky I am to still be alive. It also meant I could no longer pretend everything was okay. I had to front up to my demons, look them dead in the eye and push through.

So many people contacted me after they saw the documentary to share their stories of depression and suicide, and I realised how many of us suffer in silence or alone. It gave me the idea to take *The Enemy Within* on the road, to share with people everywhere

Here's Joe Williams, who's struggled with depression most of his life, telling it how it is. Finally, the monkey was off my back.

my battles with mental illness and my attempted suicide, and what I'd done to get through. So that's what I did, reaching out via social media and visiting schools, workplaces and communities to talk about mental health and that taboo subject — suicide. And the thing is, I got at least as much out of it as the people I talked to. Sharing my story reminded me again how lucky I am.

But when you're sharing others' pain, it can start to have an effect on you. I began to spiral down again and find myself at that dangerous crossroads of destruction, severe depression and suicidal thoughts, learning the hard way that I also needed to keep taking care of myself.

The crisis came just after Christmas, when Brodi and Phoenix were in Wagga, enjoying chilling with their cousins at my sister's house. The noise inside my head had reached its deafening worst, and I had plans of suicide screaming in my ear. When I'm talking to other people, I counsel them to reach out for help in times of darkness like this. But as much as I knew suicide should not be an option, the noise and mental pain was overwhelming.

I raced out to the back shed in a screaming mess and began scratching around the shed for a rope

When I'm talking to other people I counsel them to reach out for help in times of darkness.

of some sort so I could take my life, this time by hanging. It's not that I wanted to die; it's just that I wanted the mental pain to end.

Then, for some unknown reason, something told me to look to my right. I looked, thinking I'd find the rope I'd been searching for, but it was something very different, something that saved my life. Because when I turned to the right, I saw the microphone stand and amplifier my daughter Phoenix had been given for Christmas. Phoenix is a budding singer, and she'd been practising in the shed most of that morning and had left her music gear there. I'm thankful that a clear thought came to me, because if I'd taken my life right there and then, the first person through that garage door would have been Phoenix, looking to resume her music session.

I knew the psychological and emotional impact that type of trauma would have on a young girl, and I wasn't going to let that happen to any of my children, who I love very much. Instead, I walked back inside, grabbed my phone and made calls to get some help.

That evening I was admitted into the local Wagga Wagga Mental Health Inpatient Unit to receive more treatment and have another medication review. That stay in the mental health unit was a harsh reminder that, although I was doing good work in the mental illness space helping others, I also had to make certain I paid attention to my own mental health. If I'm not well mentally myself, then I'm no use to anyone else in the struggle.

From little things, big things grow, as brother Kev Carmody and Paul Kelly wrote. In 2015, I met an American guy called Kevin Hines. Kevin had reached out to Lauren Breen, an Australian mental health advocate who became involved in mental health and suicide prevention after her nineteen-year-old brother lost his life to suicide.

Kevin had been talking to Lauren on social media about a trip to Australia where he was planning to film his documentary *Suicide: The Ripple Effect*, focusing on the devastating effects of suicide and the tremendous positive ripple effects of advocacy, inspiration and hope, which are helping millions to heal and stay alive. Kevin needed more advocates, and asked Lauren to gather together as many Australians doing positive work in suicide prevention as she could. Then he added that he'd be in Australia to start filming the very next day. We laugh now about how Kevin gave Lauren so little time to pull together a bunch of wonderful people, but that's how a substantial proportion of Team Ripple Australia was born.

Kevin Hines — this man showed me how
to be a powerful speaker.

As soon as I met Kevin we connected like
brothers, and, since that day, my life has changed
dramatically. My initial impression was that Kevin
was a man with a deep connection to the hurt
people go through when they're experiencing pain
because of mental illness. I later learned that he'd
previously attempted suicide by jumping from

the Golden Gate Bridge in San Francisco. Since then, he's devoted his life to working in suicide prevention across the globe. Now, whenever people

From little things, big things grow, as brother Kev Carmody and Paul Kelly wrote.

talk to Kevin about the pain and anguish they feel, he shows enormous empathy and hangs on their every word — he understands the physical and mental pain they are going through.

When I told Kevin my story on the first day we met, he fought back tears. Once, when we were driving to a presentation together, I told him about a song I'd written about the day I attempted to take my life. Being a huge lover of music, I often take my guitar to schools and perform this song as part of my presentation. After listening to me sing the song about writing letters to my kids, and having so much emotional and mental pain engulf my body that all I wanted to do was end my life, Kevin started sobbing.

I understand how he feels. When people like Kevin or I hear about someone dying by suicide, it takes us back to the day we attempted to take our own lives. On the day actor Robin Williams died by suicide, I was sitting in the carpark of a school I was giving a presentation to. I sat there and cried.

Someone asked me what was wrong.

'I just heard that Robin Williams had taken his own life.'

'But how did you know Robin Williams?' they asked.

'I didn't,' I said, 'but I know the pain he was going through, I know the exact moment he decided he'd had enough, and the exact moment he flipped that coin in his mind and decided to go through with it.'

And I did, which is why I believe people could connect with me, something I still feel humble and grateful for.

17

SAYING NO TO AUSTRALIA DAY

In 2016, I was nominated for the Wagga Wagga Australia Day Citizen of the Year. When I first found out, the *Wagga Daily Advertiser* called to ask me how I felt about it. It was a great honour, I said, but also a little bittersweet as the winner would be announced on Australia Day at the Wagga community's Australia Day celebrations. And while I was extremely grateful to be recognised for the work I'd been doing around the community for mental health and suicide prevention, I felt I was caught between a rock and a hard place. Because, while 26 January is for many Australians a day to celebrate living in a free country filled with prosperity and opportunity, for Aboriginal and Torres Strait Islander people, this day marks the beginning of the invasion of our country by Europeans, it being the day that Captain Arthur Phillip sailed into Sydney Harbour and claimed possession of the land in the name of King George III.

For my people, that day was just the start of the murder and dispossession of thousands of innocent people, who were doing their best to protect their families, wives and children, in a genocide that went on for a good part of the next 200 years. All of which led to the destruction of our communities, families and our culture, and what we now call the stolen generation.

If the killing of thousands upon thousands of innocent people wasn't enough, there was the attempt to wipe out an entire race by not only killing off any people of colour, but also by stealing children with First Nations blood lines. Government men would drive into a community, collect all the children of colour and take them away from their families and place them into institutions, in order to 'make them white', which was seen as giving the natives 'a chance in life'.

I've spoken to many aunties and uncles in our communities who were part of the stolen generation. The stories from a group of aunties who were stolen and taken to the Cootamundra Girls' Home particularly affected me. The aunties were often reduced to tears as they told me how the men who worked in or around the girls' home would sneak into bedrooms at night and violently assault

While 26 January is for many Australians a day to celebrate living in a free country filled with prosperity and opportunity, for Aboriginal and Torres Strait Islander people, this day marks the beginning of the invasion of our country by Europeans.

and rape them. There were countless times when the young ladies fell pregnant as a result of rape and sexual assault. There are stories of how, after giving birth to what was then called a 'half-caste', the baby would be killed and thrown down a well on the grounds of the home. My dream is to dig into that well to free the spirits of those many tiny corpses.

There's also an infamous story about how white male settlers played a 'game' that involved burying

Aboriginal babies up to their neck, with only their heads above the surface. The men would then climb on horseback and have a contest to see how many babies' heads they could decapitate.

After reading just a couple of the many, many stories about the crimes that were committed against Indigenous people local to my area of New South Wales, you can surely understand why we First Nations people don't feel like celebrating the arrival of Captain Arthur Phillip and the First Fleet.

Many argue that we can't change the past, but we still live in a society where, despite making up only 3 per cent of the country's population, First Nations Australian men die some fifteen years earlier than non-Indigenous Australian men. I'm also a member of the race whose people have the highest suicide rate in the world, with our people eight times more likely to die by suicide than non-Indigenous Australians.

So you can see how and why it was extremely tough for me to accept that nomination and even turn up to the award ceremony. But, in the end, I came to the conclusion that I'd been nominated for the work I do with suicide prevention all year round, not just on the day of the awards.

Wagga Wagga citizen of the year.

On the day, I put on a black suit and a white T-shirt with a dreamtime message on the front. I'd cut the sleeves on the T-shirt and covered my bare arms in white ochre — a mixture of finely crushed rock and water that is used for body paint in traditional ceremony and dance. I put the rest of the ochre in a small container, and took it with me.

During the night a number of awards were announced, including one for a singing the national anthem competition. A small group of children was asked to sing the national anthem to the packed civic theatre, and the entire audience was asked to stand. While the children sang like angels, everyone in the hall stood. Everyone except for my family and me.

When it came to announcing who'd won the award for citizen of the year, my name was read out. The crowd was a few hundred strong, and they cheered loudly. I stood up and took off my suit blazer to reveal my First Nations warrior-like painted arms. It was time to paint my face. By now the audience in the auditorium was on their feet, still making loud cheers and whistles.

When I reached the podium, I could almost hear the whispers around the room, because I'd donned my traditional paint to accept my award. The mayor, Rod Kendall, congratulated me, then I took to the microphone for my acceptance speech. Even though I hadn't known I'd be receiving the award, I'd thought that, if I did, it would be a once-in-a-lifetime chance to try to educate the crowd of mostly non-Indigenous people.

I started my speech by acknowledging the traditional elders and ancestors on whose country we were gathered. I acknowledged not only the owners and custodians but also my ancestors who, some 228 years earlier, were lying down to sleep with their families, not knowing what the future days would hold. That evening, some 228 years earlier, Aboriginal and Torres Strait Island people were about to embark on a brutal war that would last until today. They would see many loved ones lost in what some call the frontier wars but what many of our people see as acts of terrorism.

I went on to talk about how many people speak of this as being in 'the past', but my dad and his brothers often had to run and hide down by the river and in creek beds when government cars approached, so they wouldn't be stolen away.

I went on to speak about how I believe the country is moving forward with regards to racism and discrimination, and how non-Indigenous Australians can learn so much from the traditional First Nations people's culture, which has lasted for over 65,000 years.

I was then reduced to tears, thanking my family — in particular, Courtney and my kids — as I believe that without them, I wouldn't have a reason to live.

The crew before our latest, Franki, arrived:
Rome, Brodi, me, Phoenix, Courtney and Ari.

In the final paragraph of my Wagga Citizen of the Year acceptance speech, I said: 'I believe the Europeans weren't sent here to kill, wipe out, torture, conquer and divide First Nations Australia. I believe they were sent here to learn from us; it has just taken us all a little longer to realise.'

I invited our community to walk together in reconciliation, and received a standing ovation.

The usual first commitment for the Australia Day Citizen of the Year is to attend a breakfast and community Australia Day Celebrations at the local Wagga Beach (which is on the Murrumbidgee

I've spoken to many aunties and uncles in our communities who were part of the stolen generation.

River) on the morning after the awards. The mayor excused me from attending — he's always been a great supporter of my community work and First Nations heritage. Instead, I drove to Sydney to spend the day of 26 January — or Invasion Day, as many of our people call it — with Brodi and Phoenix at a large First Nations festival called Yabun.

On the way to Sydney, I received a call from a local journalist in Wagga, who began by congratulating me on winning my award but quickly jumped to the point that he'd received numerous phone calls from the public, angered that I'd shown disrespect to the country by not standing for the national anthem. He asked me if this was true and, if so, what were my reasons.

I didn't shy away in my response and let him know that yes, it was true that I hadn't stood for the national anthem, and I hadn't done so for some ten years, as I don't believe our national anthem is a representation of me as a First Nations Aboriginal man living on Wiradjuri country.

I went on to tell him my reasoning was that Advance Australia Fair was a song written by a Scotsman about an English colony during the time of the White Australia Policy. When he asked me why I thought this, I told him to read all five verses of the song — there's a lot in there about Britain and 'rule Britannia'. I also stated how the line of the song 'For we are young and free' is disrespectful to our culture, because the country's first people have been here for more than 65,000 years.

Many people would not agree with my stance, but for me the big picture was about educating those who were open to learning why the national anthem is, for many of our people, a disrespectful song with no significance to us.

That day in Sydney, I had a fantastic time with family and many relatives from across New South Wales, celebrating our culture with traditional dance, food and song. I took part in a corroboree when I and my cultural brothers stomped our feet on Mother Earth, in respect, so she could feel our footsteps. We celebrated and honoured our old people, and the thousands who lost their innocent lives in the days, weeks, months and years after colonisation. I was fuelled with the power and energy of our old people.

The next morning, the local paper quoted Councillor Paul Funnell, who demanded that I hand the award back, claiming that I'd been disrespectful toward the city's top honour and the Australian public, that my behaviour was divisive and was a political stunt that was harmful for reconciliation.

My first corroboree. The connection, the positive energy created when we dance for Mother Earth is indescribable.

As well, I received hundreds of messages of support from First Nations people, family and otherwise, as well as from non-Indigenous Australians, saying that they had admired me for educating them on issues that are not often talked about in the mainstream media.

Over the following days, the media circus continued in both Wagga and parts of the rest of Australia, as Councillor Funnell and I traded views on the subject. We were invited to speak about the topic on the national television show *The Project*. Thankfully, the panel — and many viewers — agreed with me. Unfortunately, the entire country was not in my corner, and a number of family and friends contacted me, concerned about the possible impact on my wellbeing. My answer to those who called me was: 'It can't affect me if I don't pay any attention to it. I've learned over the years to build a wall of resilience to things that may have a negative impact on my wellbeing.'

The disappointing thing about the incident, though, was how it highlighted that Australia still has a long way to go if both First Nations and non-Indigenous people are to learn to walk together. I received vicious online hate mail aimed at my children (all aged under ten at the time), as well as vile racial abuse towards my parents and other family members.

But I also received huge support not only from my community but also from many people across

I believe the country is moving forward with regards to racism and discrimination.

the country, including countless aunties and uncles who stopped me in the street, at the park and at the corner shop, all thanking me for being a proud voice for our people. Through all of the drama that played out over those few weeks, the one thing I was most proud of was the message I attempted to deliver after receiving the award. It was a message of hope and reconciliation and about uniting both cultures for the future of our generations to come.

18

SPREADING MY WINGS

As a kid, I only dreamed of travelling to America, but in 2016 my dream became a reality. My first trip to the States was to NatCon, the National Council for Behavioral Health conference, in Las Vegas, Nevada. I felt extremely daunted by the thought of attending the conference, but I ended up meeting some amazing people with common views about people living well. The one thing that brought everyone together was that we were all either in recovery from a suicide attempt, bereaved by suicide, or recovering from our own mental health struggles, and the conference was filled with love, care and compassion.

We Australians had a booth, and loads of people lined up to chat with us — I am not sure if it was the accent or the fact that everyone could hear our laughter, but we were by far the most popular booth there! That week of networking led me to make more trips to the States.

My next trip over helped shape the working relationship I now have with 17th and Montgomery Productions, which is the mental health media and motivational speaking company set up by Kevin Hines and his wife, Margaret.

Kevin and Margaret invited Lauren Breen and me over for a speaking tour. Lauren is a very powerful speaker who talks from the perspective of a person who lost a member of her family to suicide, and she, Kevin and I spent ten days touring the United States. We covered eight states in ten days, delivering wellness and suicide-prevention programs to over 10,000 young people. I always get a huge rush speaking about my journey, knowing the positive impact it has on those hearing it in the audience.

It was after we got to know each other well that Kevin told me he was Native American, coming from the Arawak tribe in central America and the Caribbean. Having been adopted at a young age, Kevin didn't have much of a spiritual connection to his Native American heritage. But I feel that he and I are connected on a much deeper spiritual level, due to our shared First Nations background. I feel like a big brother to Kevin when it comes to sharing spiritual culture.

Travelling across the States, I felt a sense of growth within myself. Each time I shared my story, I opened up and showed a vulnerability and learned a different perspective of myself. And though I still experienced negative chat in my head (and I still do today), by helping others I felt a greater sense of freedom and was learning to go easy on myself from day to day.

Kevin and I not only got to share the stage but we also supported each other whenever we felt low. When we talked through our problems, the best thing was that there was no judgement because we're both filled with compassion. We both knew how crippling this illness can be. I learned so much from Kevin about how to share my experiences as a story and how the power of storytelling can impact on an individual's life.

Kevin tends to call bipolar disorder a disease, because you can recover from illnesses, but bipolar disorder is chronic. We have both accepted we will have bipolar disorder for the rest of our lives, and instead of trying to beat it — as many people try to do — we just have to manage it.

In November 2016, I found myself at a Native American powwow in Atlanta, Georgia. A powwow is similar to what Indigenous Australians call a corroboree, which is a cultural gathering celebrating and giving thanks through song and dance.

As I wandered around the powwow, I couldn't help but feel a connection. Resting my hands against the warmth of our Mother Earth, I felt the rhythmic beats of the native drums, vibrating and shaking the dry soil loose like a human heartbeat, that human being our Mother.

As the songs grew louder, the heartbeat began to penetrate my heart, and deep within my soul I felt as if I was at home sitting among my ancestors in Wiradjuri Country.

First Nations people across the globe have a connection like no other. It's hard to explain verbally — it is the getting of a hug from a stranger, someone you have never met or even laid eyes on in your entire life, yet it is a feeling of love and warmth, from someone who is family.

While I was there in the States, I decided to go

to the Standing Rock Reservation camp, which straddles North and South Dakota. I wanted to show solidarity between First Nation Australians and Native Americans, who were protesting the construction of a gas pipeline that would run directly through sacred native lands, putting local tribes' drinking water at risk.

The unusual thing about my plan was that I didn't have one. I felt no need to plan due to my firm belief

I found myself at a Native American pow wow in Atlanta, Georgia.

that my ancestors would look after me while I was on a journey so powerful and spiritual. It's hard to explain unless you have that connection. All I needed to do was organise the flight to North Dakota. I knew I wouldn't need travel from the airport to the reserve or accommodation. I just knew I'd be looked after. And I was right.

First Nations people have a connection with each other, no matter where we come from. Maybe it's due to our common experiences, the bloodshed and torture that colonisation brought us, but there is a love and connection that is unbreakable.

I haven't always felt that connection so strongly. There was a time when I wasn't as culturally strong as I am now. But, like anything, the more you

I felt as if I was at home sitting among my ancestors in Wiradjuri Country.

practise, the stronger you get. So that's what I've done, because I know it's such an important part of who I am and it's so important to my mental health.

Over the past few years, I've received a massive boost by connecting with my Aboriginal heritage and the increased closeness I feel to the spiritual side of my culture. I always knew I was Aboriginal, but being in the multicultural society we live in, I found it a little hard to connect to the roots of my culture. Now I am proud to be from a culture that has been around for 65,000 years, making it the longest continuous culture on earth.

It all started for me back when I was living in Dubbo. I was having a few spiritual moments where spirits, or some might say ghosts, would visit me during the night and pull the blankets off me and tickle my feet and ears.

This went on for about a week, so I called a couple

of guys who I knew were culturally strong and would understand what it was I was going through. Everyone has their own beliefs, but in our world, these spirits are sent to, or visit you, for a particular reason, good or bad, to give you a message. I had to find out what that message was.

I invited the men up to my house to cleanse the spiritual energy. As they walked through the house, one of the men, Uncle John Shipp, turned to me and said: 'It's about time you come bush.' What he meant was, all these years I had been searching for this

First Nations people have a connection with each other, no matter where we come from.

identity. And this was the answer — the identity had found me. These spirits were bugging me through the night to go bush and connect to the old ways.

That week, I went out into the middle of the bush. It was pitch black, no lights, as we hadn't lit a fire. Another uncle said to me (culturally, as a measure of respect, we call men who are older and more senior, uncle; or, for women, aunty): 'Are you scared of the dark or of ghosts?'

Competing in Dance Rites 2017,
Australia's national Indigenous
dance competition.

I was — growing up, we always heard stories about being out after dark.

'You come out here,' Uncle Steve said, 'to connect to the old people, the old ways. They will look after you, and you'll never have to be scared of the dark.'

Many years after that conversation, I realised he was right: I can connect. So long as I continue to connect and give respect to the old people, I'll always be safe and protected.

Once, during the final round of one of my title fights, Dad said to me: 'Let's bring this belt home for all our old people who have died before us.' I went into the final round and fought with everything I had, knowing that our ancestors had fought for us.

———

The same year, I was asked to be a keynote speaker at the World Indigenous Suicide Prevention Conference at Rotorua in New Zealand. Part of my speech was to highlight and concentrate on the importance of how connection to culture has helped in my recovery, and I played a short clip showing the power of connecting to culture through dance.

Like boxing and other physical exercise, connecting to First Nations dance and culture has enabled my mind to be free. When I connect to other people, our ancestors, the land, spirits and our ancient lore through our songlines and dance, I feel much more settled and safe.

I have travelled to many different nations and continents and would invite any non-Indigenous brothers and sisters to learn about our culture to help close the reconciliation gap, but also to learn a truly beautiful way of life. I learned recently that, out of more than 350 different First Nations languages and dialects spread across the country of Australia, traditionally there was no word for 'please' or 'thank you'. That tells me that our people never had to ask for anything, because it was expected that all possessions and belongings were to be shared. In fact, I believe our First Nations Aboriginal and Torres Strait Islander culture is the most giving, caring and sharing culture in the world.

Lately, I put out a challenge to all my non-Indigenous friends across Australia to learn about the local area they live in. I wasn't talking about their states and cities but the traditional names and areas, the language that was spoken, how the local people lived off the land and the resources they used that were local to the area.

I believe that once broader non-Indigenous society learns about and embraces our Indigenous way of living, we will see a reduction in racial prejudice and a more harmonious country.

My close friend Deanna Ledoux (right) is a native Cree woman from Canada. We met at the World Indigenous Suicide Prevention Conference in 2016 and have stayed in touch ever since. It is amazing how the native cultures around the world are so connected.

19

THE FIGHTING SPIRIT

Towards the end of 2016, Dad received the tough news that he had Hodgkin's lymphoma. The specialist said that his PET scan had 'lit up like a Christmas tree', showing a cancerous tumour behind his sternum, along with cancerous lymph nodes from his neck down to his groin.

Dad was knocked for six. But true to his fighting spirit, rather than sit and wallow in his disappointment, his first words to me after his diagnosis were: 'I won't change my lifestyle. If I sit still or slow down I will die — and I won't let that happen.'

Dad went through nine months of treatment with chemotherapy and radiation, before new scans revealed he was in remission. Throughout it all Dad didn't tell many, because he didn't want people making a fuss.

He went about his daily routine, went to work, spent time at the gym most days and ate the best he could.

During his treatment he lost a bit of weight, along with his hair and eyebrows, but the courage, strength and willpower he showed each day made me realise how much I'd learned from both my parents, just by watching them deal with their different struggles. In my eyes, my mum and dad are both modern-day warriors and they've inspired me to keep fighting my own health battles, both mental and physical.

With Dad before a fight night in Dubbo. I'm smiling, so clearly after weigh-in.

That includes a health issue I'd been gradually becoming aware of — my worsening memory. I'd been noticing for a while that it was getting worse and I'd find myself missing appointments, or forgetting to return phone calls, even missing picking up my kids when they had their bags packed to spend the night at my house. Things like that smash me emotionally inside. Writing this book at only thirty-four years of age, I sometimes can't remember what I did yesterday — including my interactions with family members and other people. It was a constant worry, and I wondered whether playing league and boxing had anything to do with it.

Then, one day at a suicide prevention conference I met the late Jackie Crowe, a commissioner with the Australian Mental Health Commission. I introduced myself and handed her my card.

'We met yesterday, Joe,' Jackie said. Apparently, the day before I'd also introduced myself, apologising that, if I forgot her name, it was probably because during my time as a boxer and rugby league player I'd copped the odd hit to the head and my memory wasn't great. We'd then had a conversation about Chronic Traumatic Encephalopathy (CTE), a neurodegenerative brain disease caused by repeated concussions or brain injuries, and commonly found among boxers and footballers. Two of the symptoms are loss of short-term memory and extreme depression.

Jackie began to educate me about CTE and its effects, and told me about the effects of traumatic brain injuries (TBI) such as concussions. Studies on retired footballers in the United States, and autopsies of those who had passed away by suicide, had revealed signs of CTE. It appeared that repeated knocks could have serious impacts on a person's mental health.

It turned out I was a prime candidate for CTE, though it can only be diagnosed during a post-mortem.

During my NRL career, I was between 78 and 82 kilograms. Often, though, I had 110–120-kilogram players doing their best to steamroll over the top of me — which is where I believe some of the damage to my brain was done. After many attempted tackles, I'd drag myself up from the ground feeling dizzy and with stars in my eyes, but the expectation was that you'd shake that off and continue with the game. There'd be times when I'd make or attempt two or three tackles in a row with my head already completely rattled and dizzy from previous knocks.

Then there was my boxing. During boxing training, we'd often go hell for leather at each other, getting knocked to the ground, but shaking it off to continue because it's 'only training'. Though boxers

Repeated knocks could have serious impacts on a person's mental health.

are rarely knocked unconscious during training, we might get a little dizzy and see stars and still be expected to keep going so as not to show weakness or let our coach down.

I had to face the fact that, while boxing played a huge part in teaching me resilience, to stay in the fight and not give up, and how to fight back against my mental demons, it had an impact on my mental ability.

Learning about the effects of CTE, and knowing the impact on my memory and mental health of the head knocks I copped playing rugby league and in my boxing, had an impact on my view about allowing my children to play contact sport. Recently I was watching my son Brodi play AFL, when he went in for a contest and had a fairly bad head clash. Brodi stood up and tried to run but he was unsteady on his feet, so I asked the coach to bring him off immediately.

I've continued to research the effects of CTE and, although I'm only in my early thirties and have plenty of sporting ability and years left in me, I've decided to retire effective immediately from all contact sports. (This is the first time I have actually written those words: 15 August 2016, 2.08 pm.)

After speaking about CTE in general conversations and on social media, numerous retired rugby league players and boxers approached me, looking for more

I hope there'll be a shift in attitudes to safety and brain health in contact sport in Australia.

information about it. They, too, were noticing the effects on their memory and mental health. I hope there'll be a shift in attitudes to safety and brain health in contact sport in Australia.

Now I am aware of it, I have begun to notice the effects. Not so long ago I'd been doing some boxing training and light sparring with novice boxers. The hits weren't very flush or hard, and yet the next morning there was a considerable slur in my words and a stutter. This was the first time I could physically see and hear the impact of very light sparring on my speech and my interaction with others. It was a scary moment.

It worries me to think that over time my memory may progressively get worse, and I'd give almost anything to get my memory back. I read that short-term memory lasts between eleven to fifteen days before it switches over into long-term memory. This could explain why I'd been struggling with my memory for the past few years.

So I began to look into ways to regenerate my brain and hopefully improve my memory. After all, the brain is a bit like a muscle, and with persistence and continual work, it should be able to regenerate.

Eventually, Clint Greenshields, whom I'd played NRL against, heard about my quest to improve my memory and got in contact. When I met up with Clint, he talked to me about brain neurophysics therapy and how it had been used successfully to retrain the neural pathways in the brain in order to regenerate the brain and memory. Clint then put me in touch with a man named Frank Cuiuli, who runs a neurophysics practice in Sydney called PIVOT.

During an appointment with Frank, he told me about the stresses athletes put on their bodies and, as in my case, brains. He explained how he prescribes specific exercises to help clear neurological pathways

Like all things in my life, I stay present, learn from each situation and continue to build.

and create new ones to get messages to the brain. In essence, Frank said that though we can't undo existing damage to the brain, we can help the brain create new neural pathways in order for the messages to get through.

I decided to give the therapy a go and, after a short but intense forty-minute session, I walked away more hopeful about regaining my memory than I had been in a long time. The first thing I noticed was that I had more physical freedom in my head and felt mentally great.

Over the next few days, I paid particular attention to things I was doing and how I was feeling. I still felt mentally well, but that may have been due to some extra cardio and running I was doing. It was about three weeks after the initial consultation that I began to notice some improvements in my memory, just small things that some people might consider as minor, but for me they were major progress. It felt like my brain was beginning to regenerate.

I am taking things slowly, and although there is progression, there have been setbacks; but like all things in my life, I stay present, learn from each situation and continue to build.

There is a long way to go, but a small start is better than no start.

20

TOWARDS A BRIGHTER FUTURE, ONE STEP AT A TIME

*O*ver the past few years, many people have told me that the work I do is courageous. My response is always that anyone can be courageous. I'm only trying to normalise the conversation about mental health and wellness in order to try to prevent suicide. We need to talk about our tough times. And anyone who does so is courageous, and they should be supported and encouraged.

In 2017, it was my turn to be supported and encouraged when I was named a finalist for the Anthony Mundine Courage Award within the National Indigenous Human Rights Awards. To be nominated and then named as a finalist in an impressive field of people was humbling enough. But after hearing the achievements of each finalist, I realised everyone there was already a winner.

The amazing Professor Chris Sarra, founder of the Stronger Smarter Institute, which works to deliver hope and better outcomes for Indigenous students, ended up taking out the award, a fantastic result. Another finalist for the award was Clinton Pryor, a Wajuk, Balardung, Kija and Yulparitja man from Western Australia. In late 2016, Clinton had set off on a walk for justice for his people. He started out from his home city of Perth and walked right across Australia to Canberra to raise awareness of the forced closure of remote Aboriginal communities by the Western Australian government and to meet with politicians to discuss the matter, as well as all the other concerns he'd gathered on his journey.

I'm a keen advocate for equality, and I've written briefly about injustice in this book. A big part of giving back is helping to empower others to achieve their dreams or goals. So, on a chilly winter's evening, I met up with Clinton to put my support behind his journey. We walked together for two days, covering approximately 70 kilometres. My time with Clinton was very special to me. We talked a lot about his journey and the fight Indigenous people have in and on our own country. We spoke about connectedness, family and our shared love for the land and culture.

Joining Clinton's walk was my way of giving back. I felt I could help his effort by spreading the word among a big non-Indigenous crowd, and it worked — Clinton and I did a live Facebook video that reached more than 15,000 people.

Walking with brother Clinton Pryor into Canberra.

Clinton's walk gained momentum as he crossed the country, sharing his story and his dreams with many, far and wide. I am thankful to have played a tiny part in that journey. Clinton hit Canberra in early September to meet with politicians, and I walked right alongside him. Together we danced around the sacred fire at the Aboriginal Tent Embassy.

There are still times when I feel suicidal and have to hang on to staying alive. Even recently, I was driving down the highway with Courtney and our child Ari in the car, when the thoughts of killing myself became loud and vivid. They were telling me to swerve into an oncoming car because my life was not worth living. Now, though, when I encounter these voices and thoughts, I ask myself: is the voice or thought talking to me real or not? It doesn't make things any easier, but if I ask myself that question it gives me time to sit back and look at the situation again rather than take instantaneous action. By getting through those times, and overcoming these thoughts and voices telling me I am worthless and don't deserve to live, I continue to build my resilience.

The first time I told Courtney about these voices, and the example of the oncoming car, she was scared big time, especially given that she and Ari were with me. But Courtney always says encouraging words of support and asks me to tell the truth about how I am feeling. Kevin Hines, his wife Margaret, and the

We need to talk about our tough times. And anyone who does so is courageous, and should be supported and encouraged.

many friends I have in the mental health space are also there to listen when I need it the most.

Mum and Dad are also great listeners and full of wise advice. So I feel like I have my support team around me.

Then there are my kids. How do I fireproof my children against mental illness? What tools can I give them? I know the effect bipolar disorder has had on me and those around me. If I'd had a chance to find out about it when I was younger, I could have learned the skills I needed to stay well or get help when I wasn't. It would have saved me quite a bit of confusion and hurt.

So I want to educate my children about the stigma of mental illness and the importance of normalising the

Now, though, when I encounter these voices and thoughts, I ask myself: is the voice or thought talking to me real or not?

conversation, to encourage them to reach out and ask me for help if they ever feel down or mentally unwell.

Recently, I started that conversation with my eldest son, Brodi, when we sat down for a heart to heart. I began by easing my way into the conversation, talking about feelings and the ups and downs of life. Then I told him about the work I do to help people who may have a mental illness, or to explain to people what it's like to have a mental illness and that it can affect anyone. I told him about some of the experiences I'd had talking in communities in Australia and in America.

Then, when I felt that Brodi was ready, I said: 'Son, did you know that in 2012, Dad had a suicide attempt?' I explained how I was feeling and told him it was nobody's fault and I didn't blame anyone for the way I was feeling.

'Yeah, I had some idea,' Brodi said. 'I didn't know what you did, but knowing the work you do now and seeing you in that film, I thought that might have been what happened. I didn't bring it up because it's too sad.'

We kept chatting away for about ten more minutes. After convincing Brodi that I'd be around a lot longer and I wouldn't be attempting to take my own life again, I started to speak about how there is

How do I fireproof my children against mental illness? What tools can I give them?

a chance my illness may be hereditary and that he should learn about it a little as he grew older.

The conversation ended on a positive note, as we talked about feelings and the best way we could support each other if we were not mentally well.

I might receive criticism for having this talk with Brodi at such a tender age, but I know how much I would have benefited if someone had told me about mental illness when I was young.

The time will come when I'll need to have the same conversation with Phoenix, Rome, Ari and my youngest daughter Franki. Until then, I'll continue to encourage all of my kids to express their feelings to me or others close to them. I always talk of the importance of expressing feelings when we aren't

I know that when it comes to explaining mental illness, it won't be a case of one fits all.

well, and I will continue to educate them about this topic until they're old enough to search and learn more themselves.

Each of my children has a unique personality, so I know that when it comes to explaining mental illness, it won't be a case of one size fits all. But I will be able to give them the right tools to deal with mental illness personally or when they are dealing with others.

Because they may learn something that saves a life — theirs or someone else's. And what can be more important than that?

21

CHOOSING A POSITIVE LIFE

If I'd made other choices in my life, I could have ended up on a very different path to the one I'm now on. But as I sit and ponder the what-could-have-beens in my life, as silly as it sounds, I'm thankful for every knock, put-down, setback and break-up that I've ever had. Because everything I've experienced has played a part in who I am today — even my attempted suicide. This isn't all down to luck, I believe, but also down to having the energy and desire to create a positive life for my loved ones and for others.

There are plenty of Australian men who have played more football games and won more boxing fights than me. But these days, that doesn't matter to me as much as committing myself to helping others, especially young people. I'm just grateful to have the opportunity to share my message with so many in Australia and the United States.

Whenever I'm giving a talk these days, I close by saying: 'Everybody has the ability to dream. But

I'm thankful for every knock, put-down, setback and break-up that I've ever had.

it's up to you how hard you chase those dreams.' At thirty-four, I'm loving life and continuing to chase my dreams.

Of course, I have bad days. I still wake up to negative circumstances and with reasons to be upset or angry, which, combined with the negative head talk and suicidal ideation, can throw me off balance. But it's in these bad days I find growth. In every negative experience I have, I search for a lesson as to why I'm feeling so bad or low. Because I know that with every lesson we can empower ourselves to be better, more well-rounded people.

Reconnecting with my culture has been one of the key parts in my mental health recovery. After all, for 65,000 years, our First Nations people didn't battle with mental illness, alcohol or drug addictions.

They respected, lived, loved and cared for each other and the land. Our First Nations culture has always been one of learning and sharing stories.

Now, no matter where I am in the world, I always keep my culture close. I can be in a different country, on a different continent, but I am a Wiradjuri First Nations man before anything else.

My journey to greater knowledge of my culture is a progressive one. Although I am merely a speck in the ocean sand, the more I become involved in my culture, the stronger mentally and spiritually I become. I feel greatly honoured to show the

Our First Nations culture has always been one of learning and sharing stories.

younger generations the importance of our cultural teachings, our dance and our beliefs, and to encourage them to hold themselves with humility in community. There are times when I've even shared my knowledge with older generations, not because I'm anything special, but because they had our culture ripped from beneath them during colonisation and the era of the stolen generations.

In fact, I believe there's something in this for all of us, no matter our race or religion. It's through connection that I see a way to end the horrific suicide rate for not only our people, but all people. Whether we connect to the land, culture, family or friends — connection keeps us alive.

The biggest lesson I've learned is to continually pay my respects to Mother Earth. She provides us with everything we need — shelter, food, water, warmth and even clothing — so we need to be respectful in all that we do every day as it can impact on Mother Earth.

I am currently travelling around the country to deliver my story and to shoot a documentary that will highlight the beauty of our traditional Indigenous culture, and how reviving some of the old ways of living will reduce our horrific suicide rates. I'm not proposing we all go back to living in the bush, but I am suggesting we adopt the old cultural values that our people have shared for eternity, of love and caring for each other, humility in community and Ngunggilanha, which means to always give to each other, to exchange things. Because if everyone is giving to each other, then everyone is receiving from each other.

This journey continues and will probably end up

being the most significant one in my life. Working with children in education, I get the chance to share what knowledge I have with both First Nations and non-Indigenous kids every single day. The most important people I get to share this knowledge with is my own children. I share our sacred lessons for them to carry our culture into the future.

As well as sharing culture, I ask everyone to be kind, respectful and humble in their journey, and

Speaking at the Koori Youth Council conference —
inspiring young leaders.

be the best possible version of themselves, whatever that may be. And I continue to honour my personal promise to myself to help others. I thank my ancestral spirits, and my higher powers that I have a beautiful fiancée in Courtney and five wonderfully talented, happy children.

In my twelve years of living a clean and sober life, I have gotten to know the real me, a man I am proud to say that kids can look up to for living a positive life and helping others. But the most important thing is that my family, immediate and extended, are proud of the man I have become and hopefully, one day,

The more I become involved in my culture, the stronger mentally and spiritually I become.

the legacy I leave. I'm not a perfect parent by any measure, I make mistakes, but I try, to the best of my ability. I may not always measure up in the opinions of my children's mothers, but so long as I know I'm doing my best, I can live with that. To know my kids love me and, even more importantly, that they know I love them is what matters most to me.

I remember a conversation with a young man in his twenties who was playing down his achievements and what he wanted to be in life. He

I share knowledge with both First Nations and non-Indigenous kids every single day.

thought that his job as a garbage collector would reflect negatively on his life. Hearing him say that took me back to some great advice I received from my sponsor when I first walked into Alcoholics Anonymous (AA). 'It doesn't matter if you're an NRL player, a pilot, a cab driver or a toilet cleaner,' he said. 'You're going to be better at whatever you do if you give away the drink.'

Today, I'm not perfect, but I try to be a mentor, an ambassador, a leader and a role model for young people — all because I choose to live alcohol- and drug-free. My life has improved beyond comparison and my sponsor's words were correct.

I am also a huge believer in personal choice. One of my very favourite quotes is: 'It is our mind that causes suffering or happiness.' In other words, we can choose to make our way out of the dark times by taking certain steps. On many occasions during my dark days, I was the one who was choosing to remain the same. I don't choose that life any more. Instead, I choose to fight out of that darkness. I choose to be happy.

If I can do it — so can you.

Ari and Franki.

PART II

DEFYING THE ENEMY WITHIN

DEFYING THE ENEMY WITHIN

When it comes to mental health issues I've walked the walk, and I know firsthand how tough the everyday battle can be with the enemy within. To this day, I still live with a deafening noise in my head and have suicidal thoughts that almost drive me to breaking point. But I know that if I take my medication and stick to my personal wellness plan and to the values that contribute to my positive brain health, I'll be okay.

In the pages that follow, you can read my thoughts on what I did and still do to survive and thrive. Of course, the following information is not a substitute for professional advice, but simply sets out what has worked for me.

It's divided into three sections:

Section 1, called First Steps, is about recognising mental health issues and reaching out for help.

Section 2, called Survive, sets out the wellness plan I use. It contains simple information about how I manage mental health on a daily basis.

Section 3, called Thrive, is about building resilience, which I believe is the key to being the best person you can be.

You can read it through from start to finish, or dip in and out as you like.

FIRST STEPS

RECOGNISE IF YOU'RE UNWELL AND SPEAK UP

For a large part of my life, I pushed the noise in my head down, because I was afraid of the stigma that came with mental illness. I was afraid that people would reject me, so I locked it up and pushed it deep down inside.

I now realise you can only push things down for so long before they start to rise back to the top. Ignoring something never addresses or fixes it. It's still there.

Looking back, I should have spoken up about my issues. For one thing, I know now that the more I speak about my mental health issues, the more therapeutic and healing it can be. In the beginning, it was tough to talk about them, and I thought everyone would judge me. But now I know that that's how depression works — it can fool us into thinking we're being judged, that no-one cares and that the world is against us. At least, that's how it is with me and many others I speak to. But the truth is, our families, friends and loved ones only want us to be safe and well, and speaking up is the first step to wellness.

Recently, I visited a psychologist in the United States, and he told me that everyone has an internal dialogue of some sort. It's just that my internal dialogue happens to be quite negative. Before I made my mental health battles public, I became convinced I had schizophrenia, and that the voices and thoughts in my head were there for a reason — I was just too scared to find out what they meant. I feel a lot better knowing that the voices and heightened thoughts are somewhat normal, but that I just need to manage them. For the most part, I've built up resilience to the voices, which prevents them from impacting on me too much.

WRAP-UP

- For a long time I ignored my mental health issues because I was afraid people would reject me. Things just got worse, so I tried to cover and hide my mental health issues with substance use and abuse. That's when I spiralled into darkness and addiction.

- When I finally told friends, family and then the community, it was a weight off my shoulders. No one rejected me and I got a lot of support, which helped me deal with my demons.

- Speaking up not only helped me, but it also encouraged so many other people to speak up and say they'd had similar experiences. Speaking up has opened up a conversation that was hidden for too long.

- The important thing is to talk to someone — a friend, family member, school teacher, sports coach, anyone — with the long-term goal of getting professional help if you need it.

DON'T BE AFRAID TO GET PROFESSIONAL HELP

It was a big step for me to build up the courage to walk into a doctor's surgery and admit I was struggling mentally and needed help, and that what I was going through was too tough for me to deal with alone. But I did it, and I don't regret it. Getting the professional advice validated what it was that I was going through; it also showed me that I wasn't alone. People were walking into doctors' surgeries every day, talking about the exact same issues that I had been hiding for years. It is also important to advocate for yourself. Speak up if you aren't feeling comfortable with medications and/or advice — it is very important to find the right professional help to suit your individual needs.

WRAP-UP

- If you think you're struggling with mental health issues, visit a doctor or the local medical centre and get yourself checked out.

- Although having great supportive friends helps, it's important to get professional help if you can.

CONSIDER MEDICATION

When I was eventually diagnosed with bipolar disorder, I was put on medication and have continued to be on it for most of the time since. Some medications haven't worked, but most of those that I've been prescribed have been beneficial to my recovery.

There were a few times when I thought I was travelling okay, and I'd take my pills inconsistently. There were other times when I neglected to take my prescribed medication altogether. It was during these times I skated a dangerous course and even flirted with death.

Now, the way I see it, if I have to take medication for the rest of my life to stay alive and live a long and fulfilling life, then that's exactly what I am going to do. I know how much medication benefits me and keeps *me* alive.

I try my best to take my medication at a similar time each day — whether it's morning or night or both — and this is having a positive effect on my mood stability.

Another important lesson I've learned is how a change in my weight can affect how well my medication works. During my boxing days, I weighed around 70 kilograms. These days I'm back to my NRL playing weight of 82 kilograms. Recently, I saw my doctor because I felt the medication wasn't working as well as it had been. I learned that putting on weight had likely impacted on the medication's effectiveness. I also learned that it can even have an impact on the *type* of medication that is prescribed. So now I keep tabs on my weight and know that if there's any significant change, I will need to get my dosage checked. The best piece of advice about medication I can give is that only a professional or expert is qualified to adjust or change your medication.

I've talked to quite a few people over the years who are against taking medication. When people tell me that, my response is that everyone is different and each medication is different for everyone. For me, medication has been a lifesaver. In fact, the two times I took myself off medication, I ended up in a mental health unit. I won't do that again.

WRAP-uP

- Everyone is different, but for me, medication really helped me to recover from mental illness.

- When I didn't take my medication or took it inconsistently, I became unwell.

- It's important to get the dosage checked every now and then. A change in body weight can affect how medication works and the dosage may need to be adjusted.

SURVIVE

HAVE A WELLNESS PLAN

I know from experience that if I'm not paying enough attention to my wellbeing, I can quite easily slip back into the darkness. I have the support of my family and friends as well as professional support from doctors, but I also need to take care of myself. So, to stay well on a consistent basis, I've put together a simple wellness plan that gives me ways to get back on track when I'm not feeling my best. This is my survival kit to get through tough times.

LOOK AFTER YOUR PHYSICAL HEALTH

Maintaining a healthy balanced diet is a crucial part of my wellness plan. I know that eating good, nutritious food every day is beneficial to my mental and physical health. For one thing, by eating nutritious food, you provide your body with the essential vitamins and minerals your brain needs to function at its best.

Physical exercise is another key part of staying well — it's been proven that exercise has a hugely positive impact on a person's mental health. Research has shown that exercising for at least 26 minutes each day is equivalent to 12 hours of positive brain health. Exercising for even longer can only have a more positive effect on your mental health.

It can be a grind, but I've set myself a training and exercise routine to get into the habit of working out. Sometimes, when my alarm goes off, I struggle to get out of bed but I know, in the end, it will make me feel better.

I believe we should be encouraging our kids to play sports so they get enough exercise to maximise their mental health. Too many young people spend too much time locked away in their bedrooms playing computer games, which I don't think can be good for their mental or physical health.

WRAP-UP

- Try to stick to a healthy diet of nutritious food and regular meals, because a good diet is good for your brain and your mental health.

- Twenty-six minutes of exercise a day can result in 12 hours of good brain health. So try to get out and get some exercise — in the gym, at the park or on the field. Take the dog for a walk or go for a run.

- If you are able, do some push-ups or go for a walk or a run. Any kind of exercise is a great way to get the blood pumping and set off the endorphin release.

LEARN AND PRACTISE MINDFULNESS

Anxiety is the most common mental illness in Australia. It affects all kinds of people everywhere. Anxiety is not just feeling stressed or a bit worried. When you suffer from anxiety, the anxious feelings don't go away. Your mind races, and you might imagine terrible things happening; you might feel breathless, and your heart rate might increase. Sometimes anxiety attacks can be so crippling you feel like you can't function.

Anxiety can be heightened by extreme thoughts about the future — I call worrying about the future a case of the 'what ifs'. What if this happens? What if that happens? What if I don't get the job? What if my child dies? What if I get cancer and die? The 'what ifs' can become so severe they cause physical symptoms, and you become convinced of the negative outcome.

But Dad once told me there is no such thing as the future — only the past and the present — and living in the present is key. By that he meant that anything we think about the future is only that — a thought!

Now, when I'm feeling anxious, I take control of my thoughts by using something called mindfulness. Mindfulness is when you concentrate only on what is happening at that moment.

A good way to focus your mind on the present is to focus on your own body. One thing I do is rub my thumb and index finger together, and to focus as hard as I can on that. I will focus on feeling the grooves of my fingerprints, the heat generated by the constant friction, fast or slow, hard or soft. This physical action enables my mind to stay in the present by concentrating on the task at hand.

Another mindfulness technique is to sit or stand and focus your mind on different parts of your body: your feet touching the soles of your shoe, your feet covered in the warmth of your socks. If you're seated, you focus on the parts of your body that are touching the chair. And you focus on your breathing — slowly in and slowly out.

Mindfulness and breathing bring your attention back to the present. And learning to live in the present enables you to build up your mental strength and not get lost in the 'what ifs'.

WRAP-uP

- Many people everywhere suffer from anxiety.

- Anxiety is when you feel so stressed or worried you might suffer physical symptoms such as breathlessness or increased heart rate, and you might feel terribly fearful or imagine terrible things happening. →

- When anxiety or a panic attack strikes, a good way to manage it is to practise mindfulness.

- Mindfulness is when you focus on the moment — the present, rather than the future or past.

- One way to practise mindfulness is to focus on your own body. You could rub your forefinger and thumb together and focus on that feeling. Or focus on your breathing.

- Exercise is another great way to be present.

LEARN AND PRACTISE THE 4, 7, 8 BREATHING TECHNIQUE

I have promised myself and my loved ones that I will not take my own life, but I still live with negative and suicidal thoughts, and it's often a huge struggle for me to forge on through the day. But the fighter in me won't let the thoughts beat me.

During one episode, I was sitting in an airport in Alabama waiting for my weather-delayed flight to be called. I started experiencing extreme paranoia, depression and frightening suicidal thoughts. My mind couldn't help wandering into the 'what ifs' — what if my CTE symptoms became so severe I could no longer function, and I lost everything and everyone I loved?

Once I was on the plane, the negative voices in my head again began bellowing at me to end my life. I knew these thoughts didn't reflect reality. So I gripped my hands and breathed in slowly using a technique that mental health advocate Kevin Hines calls 4, 7, 8:

Inhale for 4 seconds.

Hold your breath for 7 seconds.

Exhale for 8 seconds.

The effect of this breathing technique is to relax your body, lower your heart rate and focus your mind.

Often when I fly I have anxiety or panic attacks, when I become short of breath, as if there's a net around my heart and lungs constricting my breathing.

Now, when this happens, I begin by practising what I preach — mindfulness. I slowly begin to rub my index finger against my thumb, noticing that the faster I do it the warmer my fingers get. This brings my mind back to the present.

Despite practising my mindfulness techniques, soon my mind starts to frantically run through every possible worst-case scenario. I scan the air hostess up and down to see whether she is concealing a gun and wonder if she is plotting a terror attack.

I constantly peer over my shoulder, worried that the passenger behind me is about to stick a knife into my neck. I visibly shake my head, as if I'm conversing with someone or trying to shake it off and bring myself back to reality.

Now I'm worried the plane is destined to crash. Will I ever see Courtney and the kids again? Will my family know I loved them? What will my funeral be like? Will people even turn up? I'm no big deal, why would they even come?

Now, I'm back to using 4, 7, 8 — inhaling for 4 seconds, holding my breath for 7 seconds and exhaling for 8 seconds.

I'm terrified, and tears begin to well in my eyes. But on the surface I am as calm as can be. Looking at me, you'd have no idea that, on the inside, I'm a nervous wreck, gasping for air and feeling like I'm just clinging to life.

The reality is, I have no control over the plane — I only have control over how I react to these thoughts.

And none of my thoughts are real, and none of them can hurt me.

So I continue my 4, 7, 8 breathing and remember the mantra 'this too will pass'. And with time it does.

Sometimes when I'm using the 4, 7, 8 technique I count the seconds on my wrist watch, often for ten or twenty minutes. That's how long I can be in a panic. But it's this very process that contributes to my resilience.

Mindfulness and breathing are so important because many of our mental problems are heightened due to the fact we live in our heads. Our thoughts have the power to bring us down, but they also have the power to lift us back up.

If we can focus on the present and use the 4, 7, 8 breathing technique, we can manage our anxiety and negative thought processes.

WRAP-uP

- When you have a panic attack or suffer an anxiety attack, try using a mindfulness technique such as rubbing your thumb and finger together.　　　　　→

- You can also try the 4, 7, 8 breathing technique:

  Inhale for 4 seconds.
  Hold your breath for 7 seconds.
  Exhale for 8 seconds.

WRITE IT DOWN

As hard as it can be, part of my wellness plan is to write about when I'm feeling depressed, because I've found writing helps me to eventually feel better.

When you write your feelings or negative thoughts down, you see them in front of you rather than having them race around in your head. Think of them like poison — if you accidently swallow poison, your body rejects it by regurgitating it. You can treat negative thoughts and feelings the same way — by speaking them or writing them down, you 'regurgitate' them and get them out of your head and out of you.

WRAP-UP

- Write down how you feel when you're depressed.

- By writing down how you feel, it might help you to identify the next time these feelings come on again.

- Writing things down may also help you identify whether there are any external factors causing you to feel down, which you can then try to eliminate.

BREAK IT DOWN AND VALUE EACH SMALL IMPROVEMENT

At Alcoholics Anonymous (AA) and Narcotics Anonymous (NA), I learned to break everything down. There, I learned to get through tough times moment by moment; to count the minutes or seconds on a clock. This is another way of living in the present, and I know now that this has saved my life many times.

During my first few months at AA and NA,

I listened to other people in the group share their stories of being five, seven or ten years free of alcohol and drug abuse. I immediately wanted to be in those days of recovery, but I eventually realised how important it is to 'keep it in the day'. I couldn't fast forward to five years' sobriety without concentrating on being sober and drug free *today*.

Now I've lived almost twelve years in drug and alcohol recovery, and I get to share my wisdom with people struggling in their early days.

It's the same when you have frequent suicidal thoughts. You need to learn to get through them by living through each and every second. By living in the moment during that tough time, that moment, that day, you learn that every action, every thought and every breath contributes to you feeling better — or worse.

But often we expect to improve by a great margin. In fact, most people only feel better about themselves if they see a huge amount of improvement quickly.

I've learned, however, that even a small improvement of, say, 1 per cent, is worth celebrating, because I had to fight tooth and nail just to get to that 1 per cent.

One of the secrets of my recovery was learning to value small improvements. I realised I didn't need to go from zero to one hundred to improve. I only had to improve a little at a time.

Many people around the globe put enormous amounts of unnecessary pressure on themselves and others when it comes to improvement. What people need to remember is that even a little improvement is an improvement. Even if it feels like the negatives outweigh the positives, continue to build on those positives by just 1 per cent at a time. That's how I have grown to be strong and resilient in the face of adversity.

WRAP-UP

- To survive a tough situation such as addiction or suicidal thoughts, you need to break it down into minutes or seconds.

- Each second or minute you survive is an improvement on the previous second or minute.

- Don't pressure yourself to improve by 100 per cent. →

- Even a 1 per cent improvement is worth celebrating.

- Each 1 per cent builds on the previous 1 per cent, until you one day discover you've made big improvements.

FOCUS ON WHY YOU STAY CLEAN

Think of your favourite treat, whether it's chocolate, cake, a soft drink or a packet of chips. Think of how that sugar rush gives you an instantaneous craving for more and more, to the point you might make yourself sick.

Now think of how those treats, when they enter your body, set off a chemical reaction in your brain to act on impulse and participate in silly behaviours. And imagine you have so many of these treats that you completely forget what you did the day before. Also, to make things worse, these treats might be illegal and may cause death in some extreme cases.

This is what happens with alcohol and drugs. And because of a chemical imbalance in the brain, many people are more prone to becoming addicted to alcohol or drugs.

Now, because alcohol is a legalised drug, I see it as the number one drug that is killing our communities.

At the time of writing this book, I'm approaching twelve years clean and sober from alcohol and drugs, which I believe is one of my greatest achievements. But I know that even though I'm in recovery, I still battle alcoholism. At some point of any day, I'll want drugs or alcohol. Some people call this a substance use disorder.

There have been many times in my life when I've wanted to pick up a drink and go back to my days of partying with party drugs. I still carry a genetic disposition towards alcoholism, but that doesn't mean I must drink.

I take my substance use disorder seriously, because if I give in to the desire to pick up a drink or take a drug again, I may spiral into depression and risk suicide.

There are still times when I feel down and out, and want to throw everything away because the world seems too tough to handle and everything seems to be going against me. But these days I know that these tough times will pass, as they always have.

Some years ago, when I was helping a close friend called Jody through her personal journey of recovery, she said: 'This too shall pass'. Since then, we've both had that saying tattooed on our bodies, because, in our experience, no matter how tough the situation, it passes.

I'm not pretending it's been easy. I know I'm a recovering addict, and that risk of addiction is forever tapping me on the shoulder to remind me it's there. I still struggle when it comes to pain medication, and I have to be extremely careful about taking any type of prescription medication, checking with the doctor to make sure the medication is not a mind-altering substances. I can't take any mind-altering substance because there's the risk they could take me back to the days of being a barely functioning addict, of wanting the thrill of the chase and the feeling of medication. Even when someone like me knows I shouldn't be taking something, the cunning mind of a recovering addict will convince me it will be okay.

When that happens, I remind myself why I quit alcohol and drugs — to improve my life, but also to be a role model for my kids, to show them you don't need any type of substance to live a happy life and have an enjoyable time. The truth is, all the trophies on the shelf couldn't compare to knowing that my kids don't see their dad drinking. I'm so very proud that my children have never seen me drink alcohol. Hopefully they never will. But it's one day at a time.

WRAP-UP

- Many people think they have to beat addictions. But most people are genetically predisposed for addiction, and we carry these genes our entire lives.

- You don't have to beat addictions. You just have to learn to manage them.

- There have been many times when I could have turned to alcohol or drugs to silence the voices or get through a tough situation.

- When that happens, a voice in my head will tell me it will be okay to have a drink or take a drug. But I know that it won't.

- When that happens, I remind myself why I quit alcohol and drugs.

THRIVE

BUILD UP YOUR RESILIENCE

Whenever I lost a boxing match, I generally had to wait hours, weeks and sometimes months for my next fight and next chance to win. In those months between a loss and the next fight, doubts would overcome me. To keep going forward towards my new goal, I needed to build resilience. I learned that repetition of thought and action was my best friend in terms of keeping on track and staying resilient.

I learned to break the many months, weeks, days and hours into the smallest of fragments. And I would tell myself that anything I'd done in the past would impact on what I was achieving now, and anything I did now would impact on my achievements tomorrow. Every small step counted, and each could make the difference.

Coping with mental illness requires a similar approach. And building resilience is vital if you're not only to survive but thrive. I've learned that improvement isn't measured in material possessions or numbers, but by tiny degrees, one step at a time. I've learned to breathe through those dark times, and in breathing through those times of despair I've learned to improve second by second, every minute of every hour of every day. Slowly, the minutes turn into days, the days into weeks, the weeks into months and I'm on track to becoming the best possible version of myself. In learning resilience through tough times, I've learned to not only survive, but thrive. Here are some of the things that have helped me build resilience and helped me thrive.

EMBRACE YOUR FEARS

Our deepest fear is not that we are inadequate.
Our deepest fear is that we are powerful beyond measure.
It is our light, not our darkness, that most frightens us.
We ask ourselves, 'Who am I to be brilliant, gorgeous,
*   handsome, talented and fabulous?' Actually, who are*
*   you not to be?*

Marianne Williamson, *A Return to Love*

I first heard this quote when I saw the movie *Coach Carter*. I didn't quite understand it at the time, but a few years on, having experienced my fair share of disappointments and setbacks, it started to be a little more relatable.

Like everyone, my fears and insecurities would pop up, whether in a rugby league game, a physical confrontation in the ring, doing the hard yards in the gym, or facing situations in everyday life.

Thanks to my parents, I'd been blessed with athletic ability. But my deepest fear, even as a kid, was what would happen if I tried my absolute best and fell short? I was so afraid I'd be lost and emotionally hurt, I was too scared to try my absolute best. It's true that throughout my entire NRL career I had the attitude of just doing enough to get by, because I was afraid of doing my best — and failing.

Occasionally, I'd face my inner fears when I was playing league — times in the final minutes of a game when the team needed a big play to get us over the line. One such time was when I was playing for the Sydney Roosters in the Jersey Flegg Grand Final. The scores were tied with approximately two minutes left on the clock. It was a grand final, I had to stand up so I called for the ball 35 metres out from the opposition line and hit the sweetest field goal I've ever kicked in my career. We won the game by one point. I did it that day, but so often I was too hesitant to go the extra mile.

I also still carry the burden of knowing I hurt many people in the past due to my fears. In my personal relationships, I never gave myself entirely to the woman I loved for fear of getting hurt. This was not fair on my partners, who had given me their complete loyalty and trust.

So everyone has fears and insecurities. It's how you deal with them that counts. And when I was younger, I didn't deal with them well.

These days, when I feel fear, I always remember my dad's story about the little boy or girl inside us all, and how we need to take that little boy or girl by the hand and face our fear together. 'Lead that little boy, be his guiding light, together as one. Together you can conquer any obstacle you face,' Dad said. And that's what I do. I take the little boy inside me by the hand and together we move forward, through the fear.

Boxing helped me develop the mental strength to confront my fears. In the boxing ring I learned to give my best, to never give up and to fight to the finish. I see it like this: every single time I step inside the boxing gym, I am asked the questions that bring out the little boy inside me. Every time things get physically hard in training, it tests me mentally.

Once upon a time I wasn't able to stand strong in those tough situations, and I'd run and hide. Now, when I search deep inside myself, I like the person I find. I am a strong warrior, happy to guide that little boy into the deep and come through to the other side.

So often it's not physical obstacles that cause people to fall short, but mental factors. By surviving physical challenges, you build mental toughness. Since I took up boxing, I'm always looking for new physical challenges, because they test me mentally as well.

I am still tested by my fears, which continue to haunt me. But every day is a fresh start to build on what I overcame the day before. And fears are only fears — they're not reality.

WRAP-UP

- Learn that each fear is just a thought.

- Break each thought down and then slowly begin to chip away at it to overcome it.

- Physical challenges help you grow stronger mentally.

LET GO OF EGO

It's tough to keep control of your ego, which could be defined as your sense of self-importance. Well, it certainly was tough for me, especially during my league career, when, it's fair to say, the bright lights got to me. I was living in Sydney, and while I was still in contact with some of my friends from home, football and training consumed a lot of my life. And with all the attention from the public, even the media, I found it tough to stay grounded.

An inflated ego can affect our ability to see things with a balanced perspective, and that can impact badly on us and other people. It's your ego that most fears failure and wants to give up at the first sign of difficulty or struggle. So if you have an inflated ego, it's harder to build resilience.

After some self-reflection, I have come to the conclusion that some of the worst moments in my life came down to one person carrying too much ego, and in the majority of cases that person was me. Whether I was constantly going out and partying, drinking and taking drugs, or walking away from the mothers of my children on two separate occasions, it was because I lived in a fake world filled with ego.

In my opinion, ego can cause a person to act in ways they don't really want to. My bipolar disorder diagnosis helped me to understand that my ego usually kicked in during my manic periods. When I was manic, I would chase the high for days, at first through alcohol and drugs, and then via the nightclub scene, which gave me a thrill that also fed my ego.

Ego can also lead to schoolyard bullying, competition between friends, and disagreements between nations. Many of the most powerful politicians have outsized egos. If only our leaders were driven by love, compassion and respect instead of ego, the world might have fewer wars and less terrorism. In fact, I believe that if people could let go of ego, we'd see a happier, kinder, more loving world.

WRAP-UP

- There are two emotions in every person's heart — love and hate.

- Love fuels compassion — hate fuels ego.

- Your ego fears failure, and if you fear failure, you will struggle to build resilience.

REMEMBER IT'S NEVER A LOSS — ALWAYS A LESSON

We all know people who are suffering, whether it be with illness, financial breakdown or the pain of losing a loved one.

And many of those who we think are successful have a backstory of physical and emotional hurt, sadness, grief or loss. But what makes them different is their ability to seize the moment, despite their struggles, and turn a defeat into an opportunity rather than a setback.

I've certainly peeled myself off the canvas many times in my life — in rugby league, in boxing, in my relationships and, probably most significantly, following my suicide attempt. But no matter how many times I have been knocked down, almost counted out, and decided I have had enough, I've somehow found the will to get back onto my feet.

It was difficult to bounce back from the breakdown of my relationships with the mothers of my first three children. Though a breakdown in understanding with someone you've loved is painful in itself, the greatest pain for me was the separation process, because it resulted in my kids' growing up in a household without their father. Now, I comfort myself by saying that, if things had turned out differently, we wouldn't have our little crew and I wouldn't have met my fiancée Courtney, and our ratpack wouldn't be complete without our two youngest, Ari and Franki.

Accepting defeat and failure gives you the resilience to bounce back, as you recognise that today's defeat could be tomorrow's success.

WRAP-UP

- It's not failure that's important, but how you deal with it.

- Try to see defeats or failure as an opportunity to learn something new.

- Try to see the positive in a situation rather than focus on the negative.

IGNORE OTHERS' LABELS AND BE PROUD OF WHO YOU ARE

So many people today worry about what other people think, so much so that sometimes it can affect their mental health. I believe young people in particular can suffer from low self-esteem, due to both what they see as society or peer-group expectations and the expectations they put on themselves.

People seem to feel the need to compete against each other more these days. Everybody wants to be better than someone else, when all they need to be is the best possible version of themselves.

People also seem to be obsessed with labels. A

label is something society puts on a person in a way that makes them think they should fit that label. But the truth is, only that person has the right to choose who they are — black, white, sportsperson, smart, dumb, ugly, attractive, tall, short, fat, skinny etc.

In my life, I've been labelled many things, but I now realise I'm only those things if I *choose* to believe them. Some of those labels I choose to accept, but many I choose to reject.

I'm somebody who *chooses* to be a little left of centre and out there. Why? Because I like to challenge people's perceptions. I like to break the mould and change people's expectations of who I am or who I should be. For example, when I was a schoolboy rugby league player, I got up in front of 1500 students at my all-male Catholic school assembly and belted out a love song by Joshua Kadison on acoustic piano. Afterwards, I was teased and ridiculed behind my back for being a 'nancy boy' singer — until I ran out and captained the school rugby league team, scored some tries and kicked a few goals. Wait, a 'nancy boy' singer isn't supposed to do that! Well, who says?

When I tell people I have Aboriginal heritage, there's often a fixed perception of who I am and how I should look, talk, act and behave. Again, I like to blow that perception away and lead people to have a different perception of how Indigenous people should be. Because these perceptions are nothing but *labels*.

When I talk to people about being a First Nations man or 'Blackfulla' — as many of us describe ourselves — people often react by saying, 'But you're not black.' Rather than take offence, I see this point in the conversation as one where the real reconciliation process begins. It's a chance for me to educate people on what has happened to our people since colonisation. Many of our ancestors were very dark in colour, and in the early days we were exactly that, black. But years of breeding with non-Indigenous people, both willingly and, in too many cases, unwillingly — to try to breed out the bloodlines of our people — gave us lighter-coloured skin.

When it comes to society's labels, I am many things. I'm a First Nations Australian Aboriginal man as well as a father, fiancé, friend, sportsperson, recovering alcoholic and drug addict, mentor, author, activist, truth talker, university student, lover of lollies, mental health and suicide advocate, left-handed, musician, singer, runner, personal trainer, life coach, charity ambassador, fashion designer, cake maker, bipolar disorder sufferer, Holden-driving fisherman who lives with mental illness and frequent suicidal ideation, former NRL player, and professional boxer who loves watching ballet.

Above all of that, I'm me, Joe Williams. So often we look at the colour of someone's skin, their interests, their sexuality, their job or title, to define who they should be, because that's how people want us to be.

But at the end of the day, the only person you should be is the person you *want* to be. Ignore or shed others' labels and start living the way *you* want to live, because *you* are in control of your own destiny — not society. When you're buried, you're the only person in that box and all the opinions about how you lived your life won't be important any more.

In particular, labelling someone as mentally ill can be one of the most demeaning things anyone can do. Because labels like that lead to stigma and discrimination.

For example, why is it that when we hear of a violent crime, people expect the perpetrators to have a mental illness? When we see or hear of a mental health facility, we think the people inside are 'locked away', and are insane, nuts, crazy. When our sports stars commit a crime or show negative behaviour, we blame mental illness.

This is why so many people hide mental health and substance use disorders, because they are judged negatively by others. The media could have a positive effect on public perception if they stopped reporting only negative stories about mental illness.

I'm an individual who battles depression on a daily basis, and who experiences negative and suicidal thoughts, and I've been quite open about my struggles with mental illness. I am someone who lives and breathes a positive lifestyle, and tries to help people in times of crisis. I'm often described as someone who is inspirational to people in times of need. One would say I am a positive person.

And yet a person like me, who struggles with a mental illness, is often described, judged and talked about in a negative manner.

There is certainly a stigma around mental illness, but there's also discrimination. Many brothers and sisters who battle their inner demons are discriminated against because they suffer from illness. We don't see people discriminated against when they have heart disease or cancer, because they're physical illnesses.

But, too many times, we put down, talk negatively about and even discriminate against those who have a mental illness.

Many people have very little idea just how closely related addictions and mental illness are. In fact, many mental health professionals believe addictions are in fact a mental illness called substance use disorder. Some people think that too much drug use will lead to mental illness. But in many cases, people use drugs and alcohol to mask mental illness. I know that this was the case with me and others I've come into contact with and tried to help.

It's so bad in some cases that people with substance use disorder are so discriminated against they end up in prison, often with little to no rehabilitation.

But would we ignore a physical illness or lock someone away for liver, heart or lung disease? Of course not. So why do we often ignore people's mental illness and even punish them for it?

I believe that both the media and we as a community need to look at how we perceive and depict people with mental illness. In doing so, we need to look at the language we use when talking about or describing mental illness.

I am an individual who is lucky to have caught

my addiction and alcohol abuse problems at an earlier than average age, and learned to keep my mental health demons at bay, but I ask you this: think about what you would do if you answered the door to me (knowing my story) and I was asking for help while I wasn't feeling mentally well, and if you answered the door to a homeless, alcoholic, drug addict in a bout of depression asking for advice or help. Would you treat us both with the same amount of concern, safety and care?

The answer should be 'yes', you would treat us both the same, the only difference is I have a home to live in and I know how to manage my mental health, whereas the other person doesn't.

So ignore the labels other people give you. You're not a label, you're the person you want to be. I know that when I started to live by this motto, my mental health began to improve. No longer was I letting exterior factors get me down. No longer was I trying to live up to others' expectations of who I should be or who they wanted me to be. I was just me. Joe. The person I want to be.

WRAP-uP

- Let the only label you carry be your name.

- Don't let others' labels define who you are or who you are supposed to be.

STARE DOWN RACISM OR DISCRIMINATION

I've encountered racism and discrimination throughout my life, and dealing with both has helped me build my resilience. I've lost count of the times in my life when, due to the colour of my skin, I've been victimised, racially abused and discriminated against.

Even now, I still come up against subtle racism, which people tend to pass off as a 'joke' or let slip with a shake of the head. What I say to bystanders of racism is: what you ignore, you accept.

Everyone is affected by racism or discrimination differently, and everyone deals with it differently. Dad's advice was that it's better to beat a bigot through intelligence rather than physical violence and fist fights, and that helped me build up my long-term resilience in the face of racism. I realised that, yeah, I could get into a fight and maybe even win, but if I punched someone in the mouth, nobody learned anything. At least if I tried to beat someone with intelligence, I was also educating the person who was trying to bully or discriminate against me and nobody would get hurt.

The racist person may become extremely frustrated, but humiliating someone about their lack of intelligence or education is a great way to reverse the power dynamic. Now I counter racism by being educated about where I am from, the true history of this country and the struggle Indigenous people have endured to be where we are.

WRAP-UP

- Learn about your culture.

- Learn about your people.

- Anger doesn't solve racism or discrimination. Racism and discrimination hurts, but try to use the situation as an opportunity to educate.

CONNECT WITH YOUR CULTURE

Wiradjuri is the name for Indigenous people like me from central New South Wales. Collectively, all New South Wales First Nations people are called Kooris. In most of Queensland they are known as Murris; in parts of Western Australia the term Ngoonga and Yamatji is used; in South Australia, Nunga; in Tasmania, Palawa; and in the Northern Territory a few different names are used.

Research has shown that Aboriginal people have been roaming the land for 65,000 years, but our cultural stories tell us we have existed since the beginning of time. It's in our stories that we learn our lessons of life — stories like the creation, the rainbow serpent weaving his way across the land, creating the hills, mountains, rivers, plains and waterways.

It's been said that, before colonisation, our people did not have mental health problems. They did not know suicide, and everyone was loved, nurtured and cared for. There were rules and laws within our communities, which were called our lore. Living close to lore enabled our spirit to be in line with our past, present and future. Our lore was practised, learned and lived, with traditional rituals and ceremonies carried out that kept everyone spiritually safe and connected.

Our belief was that, as long as we lived by and practised our lore, we wouldn't be punished physically, emotionally or spiritually. Everyone obeyed the lore for fear of being cast out of the community — community love and respect was always at the forefront. If we stayed in line with the lore, within our community, we stayed connected physically, spiritually and emotionally — which kept our mental health strong.

Our lore and culture have survived since the beginning of time by living with respect, humility and love. And I believe there is something we can all learn from this. By returning to our traditional people's values of love, care, respect and humility, we will deliver greater rewards for everyone. In traditional times, there was never any greed, the only emphasis that had value was how much you loved and respected someone. No social media, no bullying, no drugs, no alcohol, no unhealthy foods, as everything came from Mother Earth. And definitely no racism.

We may not be able to bring back all of these past cultural practices, but we can most definitely live by the cultural values that kept everyone spiritually in line. They are love, care, respect and humility.

For me, reconnecting to my First Nations culture has been the most significant thing in my mental health recovery. This connection to culture has had an enormous impact on my wellbeing over the past few years. I still have my down days, where I can easily slip back into the depths of depression; however, the more in tune I am with my culture, the better I feel, emotionally and spiritually. The more respectful I am towards Mother Earth, the animals and waterways, the clearer I am mentally.

It's not always easy for First Nations people to connect with their culture — across the country, many struggle because their elders may not be around any more, or they too weren't taught about culture because it was banished or forbidden due to colonisation.

But it is possible to rediscover your culture — you might look into the local art of the area, or learn some of the old ways. It won't always just fall into your lap — sometimes you have to search for it.

WRAP-UP

- Learn about who you are by connecting to the old ways, the elders and the country.

- Once you find and learn that connection, share it.

- Be proud of your people and your history.

ACCEPT WHAT YOU CAN'T CONTROL, AND FIND SERENITY

One of the most important things I learned in Alcoholics Anonymous was the Serenity Prayer, which is about accepting the things you cannot change and having the courage to change the things you can — and knowing the difference between what you can and what you can't control. The first verse goes:

> *God, grant me the serenity to accept*
> *the things I cannot change,*
> *The courage to change the things I can,*
> *And the wisdom to know the difference.*

That prayer put me on a path to training my mind towards acceptance, to understanding to control the controllable and let go of the rest.

Now, when I'm driving myself crazy worrying about all the bad things that could happen, I now tell myself: 'I can't control certain things that happen to me in my life — but I can control how I react to them.'

For so long I'd get myself into a knot worrying about the outcome of an event. I'd struggle with so many situations in my sporting and rugby league life because I believed the negative outcome more often than the positive. I was beaten in the mind before I was beaten physically. Sometimes I would make myself so anxious about what was going to happen I would be physically sick and lock myself away in a room for hours, not speaking to anyone.

It was only when I learned my number one coping mechanism for my fight with mental illness that I started to get well — and that coping mechanism was that I could only control the controllable.

I often encounter situations where I have to put this to the test. When I learned to live in the present moment and control only the things I can control, things started to improve.

So often I would push the hard and negative times away, down or to the side, and when it all became too much it began to overflow into my physical behaviours.

With the negative situations and outcomes, I would begin to question myself, saying things like: Why me? I'm a good person? What did I do to deserve this?

But asking these questions didn't change the situation that I was in. In fact, often it just compounded it.

What I didn't see was that negative things happen to other good people, too — not just me. Many negative situations I encountered in my life often led me into a deep and dark depression. I found that the key to moving forward was to reconcile myself with my past, find inner peace within myself and build resilience in what I was doing in the present, which would put me in a beneficial place for the future.

It is better to be a person of understanding and acceptance than someone always searching for answers. I have found that the answers come when you find peace and a still mind.

To be able to have a still mind takes great practice and patience. I had to learn how to switch off my mind. There was so much craziness and chaos in my head, I had to learn to switch off my mind. I found meditation and mindfulness techniques great for this, particularly when I'm not feeling mentally well.

As well as meditation and mindfulness, you can introduce practical behaviours to your life to help gain a quiet mind. These are the sorts of things nearly anyone can achieve — exercise, reading, having conversations with people about common interests, loving your friends and family, showing them you care.

I have found that people who are struggling for certain answers in life often know the answers to their own problems, but hearing it from someone else helps confirm it.

When I find myself searching for answers, I think about what advice I would give to my best friend, child or friend when they are confronted with the same crisis.

My life became a lot more positive when I learned to control the controllable, and to let go of what you have no control over. By not worrying about the things I have no control over, I find the outcome sorts itself out in time.

BE GRATEFUL AND COMPASSIONATE

One thing I have learned over the years is to be grateful for my life. Every day I have the chance to keep the promise I made to myself to have a positive impact on people's lives, including my family.

My parents raised us kids to be grateful for what we had, because someone, somewhere, was always doing it that little bit harder. For as long as I can remember, I had always felt bad for having certain things that were better or more expensive than what other people had. To this day, material things mean nothing to me. I don't need flash houses, cars and boats. As long as I have a roof over my head, clothes on my back and food in my stomach, nothing else matters.

To me, good health, a caring heart and compassion for others are much more important. Take all the material possessions away, and it's a person's soul that matters.

So no matter what happens, I try to be grateful, and it's a good habit to get into. For example, if I'm cold, or I'm hungry, I remind myself to be grateful for the clothes on my back, the shoes I'm wearing and the fact I have feet to put my shoes on, and the meal I last ate and the one I know I'll be eating soon.

If you try hard enough, you can find gratefulness in almost every situation you encounter in your life. I really learned gratefulness from a bunch of kids in a community in a remote part of the Northern Territory. The kids were over the moon because they got to kick the bladder of a footy around. The young people in that community didn't have much, but they were grateful for what they had.

I've learned that everything we need in our life, Mother Earth provides, so anything we have on top of the barest necessities we should be grateful for.

Compassion is another quality I try to practise in my daily life. I believe that everyone we meet may be facing a battle we know nothing about and may act the way they do for a reason, so, as much as possible, I try to show everyone compassion, love and care. I work with a lot of young people in juvenile detention centres, and while I don't support criminal activity, I try to put on my compassionate hat when I talk to these young people to find out why they have ended up where they are. Many of them have been detained for crimes such as stealing, or breaking and entering an occupied home. I asked two young men what led to them stealing in one case and breaking and entering in the other. Both told me they'd not had a meal in days and had committed crimes to get food. I don't agree with their actions. However, I do show compassion in the face of their misjudgements.

WRAP-UP

- Try to treat every person you meet with compassion and without judgement.

- It's easy to judge someone by their behaviour, but instead, judge them by the traumas they have experienced, which in most cases are the cause of the behaviour.

LIVE A LIFE OF VALUE, AND SHOW LOVE, RESPECT AND HUMILITY

I greatly admire boxing coach Billy Hussein. He's a man I consider a brother. Billy is hugely successful as a coach, not only, I believe, because of his boxers' talent and work ethic but also because, outside the boxing ring, he instils in his boxers an attitude to life.

The first few times I trained under Billy I noticed that every time one of his boxers came into the gym, they walked around to every single person and shook hands and asked them how they were doing. Now, you might not think that sounds like much, but to me it speaks of the humility of every fighter that Billy Hussein trains. Billy doesn't just train these guys to be boxers, he trains these guys to be humble young men. In Billy's gym there are values, and no matter who you are or where you sit, everyone lives those values, not just because they're part of the rules but because they are good values to have in life.

One day I was speaking to Billy on the phone about people's culture. By this I don't mean my culture as a First Nations Aboriginal man, or Billy's culture as a devout Muslim. Instead, we were talking about the culture people have in the way they carry themselves.

It got me thinking: there's a particular culture I have in my life — standards I accept for myself and which I don't let myself down by lowering them. I have lost many friends and people I considered close because I don't like having people with negative behaviours in my life. I gave away alcohol twelve years ago because it was having a negative effect on me, and I don't want that lifestyle for my kids.

Billy talked about how he sets his fighters up mentally for a lifestyle that they can be proud of — one of humility, poise and value. Billy provides his fighters with a culture to be better people.

For me, being a better person is trying to always show others love, respect and humility. This helps keep me mentally well. No matter the situation, I have learned to demonstrate my love. There are many circumstances where it is difficult to show love to people, but there are only two different emotions in our heart when it comes to thinking about others or situations we encounter. Those two emotions are love and hate. If you walk around with hate in your heart, then you will be negative, bitter and nasty. If you let love rule your heart, you will find more joy, appreciation and acceptance. Love beats hate every single time.

I try to show respect for everyone I encounter in life. I may not agree with some people, but I respect that they are on their own journey, and it's not for me to judge their actions when I have no idea of their personal circumstances.

And I try to be humble wherever I go. Because no matter where I am or who I am with, there's always somebody watching.

WRAP-uP

- Being a role model doesn't cost any money, but you become extremely valuable.

- In a society littered with negativity, be that person people want to be like.

- Do the best you can every single day — no one is perfect, but be the best version of you that you can be.

BE POSITIVE AND SURROUND YOURSELF WITH POSITIVE PEOPLE

I'm someone who doesn't like being around alcohol, not because I don't drink it but because I believe it's a poison that does more harm than good in many communities throughout Australia. In fact, alcohol and drugs have caused major havoc in many of our First Nations communities, which has led us to have high alcohol and drug dependency and too many of our children born with foetal alcohol syndrome. As a result, I try my best to model a behaviour that

I would want my children to be proud of. I make sure that I am never seen in a picture with alcohol, cigarettes or anything that will be viewed negatively. As I've said many times, you can't be a role model just from 9 to 5 or during work hours — being a role model isn't a job, it's a lifestyle.

I'm proud that I'm a man of honour and, when people talk about me, for the most part, it's in positive terms. I am also proud to be considered a role model for youth, but not because it makes me look good. What I do and why I do it, especially in a public arena, is to encourage not only younger people but all people to always display a positive image of themselves.

But I have had 'friends' come and go, due to my lifestyle. Having these friends, acquaintances and even family drop out of your life makes you realise who is important and who is a support for you in your positive choices. And at the end of the day, if these people choose to stay away from you because you like a cleaner lifestyle, then that reflects more on them than you.

By only hanging around positive people with a positive attitude, you begin to live a positive life. It's infectious — the more people see it, the more people want it. That's how you create a positive culture.

WRAP-uP

- Try to make positive choices.

- Surround yourself with positive people.

- Positivity is contagious.

FIND A MENTOR

I've been fortunate to meet and spend time with many great people during my life. There have been sports stars, political activists, musicians and family members who have come into my life and taught me lessons that will last me a lifetime. These are the people I call mentors, people who had more experience in a situation than I did, and gave me the guidance and help I've needed through my life. Mentors don't always have to be an older person, but I must say it helps, as they usually have the greater life experience.

Mentors want people to be like them, show the behaviours they show, and interact in a positive manner in community. You can see a mentor by the way they carry themselves in community. Mentors are usually humble yet motivating, positive yet truthful. Model those traits.

It is these behaviours I try hard to shadow every day.

I've been extremely lucky to have had some great mentors who have helped shape the person I have grown into. They include my parents, sports coaches, school teachers, some of my teammates and now my partner, Courtney.

MY PARENTS

When it comes to who has had the most influence on me, of course I can't go past my parents. As well as sacrificing a lot so I could pursue my dreams, they were both integral to my development as an adult. Learning from their different approaches to parenting has enabled me to be the best father I can be for each of my kids today.

Mum and Dad have very different ways of showing love, care, empathy, compassion and discipline. Mum always had our backs as kids. She was always the nurturer, showing tender loving care for me and my siblings, while also ingraining discipline into us from when we were very small. It was Mum who I and my brother and sisters would cling on to when we were sick as kids, or upset for some reason, whether it was from having our feelings hurt or injuring ourselves playing sport. Mum always held our family together. There were many times when our family was burdened with financial heartache, but Mum never showed stress or worry — she always just got it done.

During my NRL playing career, I would call Mum in tears wanting to move home, or for a loan of $20 to get the kids a feed for dinner. Throughout my entire life, Mum has been my emotional rock, particularly during my divorce from Suzie and my break-up with Tegan. Mum was always there to give sound advice or wipe away tears.

Mum taught us all so much, but for me, the most important thing I learned from her was to always put others before yourself. Countless times in my childhood, Mum went without just so we kids could do what we wanted to do or achieve what we needed to achieve.

My relationship with Dad was very different. He's also always had my back but, never one to talk about feelings and sometimes stern, Dad has his own unique way of delivering a message when giving advice. Both as stubborn as each other, Dad and I had countless arguments when I was younger, butting heads over differing opinions. This was especially the case during my sporting career, whether Dad was giving positive criticism of my game as a league player or a harsh opinion during my boxing career. That said, he was my best motivator in sport.

Despite only completing high school up until Year 8, Dad is by far the most intelligent man I have ever met. As an adult he has done further education, and it amazes me that for every single exam he has sat in his working life, he has been extremely disappointed if he didn't receive 100 per cent. Now I'm in my thirties, Dad is someone I consider more of a best mate than a father, and I really value his wisdom, which is something he has in abundance.

In our culture, young boys can only be taught certain lessons by their biological father or uncles. Dad's father passed away when he was just nine years of age, so his entire life he was looking for that cultural leader to teach him lessons. I realise now he sought out these lessons through other means, through life experience and learning from others.

It was Dad who taught me certain Indigenous lessons and protocols, without which I wouldn't be who I am today. It worries me that, not always living with my kids, I'm not able to provide as much cultural guidance to my sons as Dad gave me. Phoenix's mum can teach her lessons, but Brodi and Rome can't get the lessons from their mother, or their non-Indigenous stepfather.

Dad has been the biggest inspiration for getting through tough situations. Dad's never-give-up, grit-your-teeth attitude in tough situations, physical or mental, never ceases to amaze me. When he was diagnosed with lymphoma, his first words were: 'Oh well, what do we have to do to beat it? Whatever it is, sign me up.' That's my dad.

COURTNEY

I've mentioned a few people who have been very influential in my life, but I wanted to dedicate a separate piece to Courtney Merritt.

I met Court when I already had three children. The most amazing thing about her is not only the way she treats me with love and respect, but also how she cares for all my children, not just her own.

I think I'd been searching for a woman who treated and cared for her family the way Mum did ours — and with Courtney I believe I have found that. Courtney is like Mum in so many ways, always putting others before herself, never making a fuss, just getting things done. She's a great role model and mentor.

But her care for my kids has always been the clincher. The love she shows all of my children is inspiring.

ARTHUR BEETSON

Whenever I'm asked who have been the biggest influences in my sporting career, I name the two men I have loved like fathers — rugby immortal Arthur Beetson (Beetso) and my first boxing coach, Johnny Lewis.

I was too young to remember Beetso as a player, though I once heard him described as a halfback in a prop's body, having silky smooth skills and great body movement for such a big man. Many years later, someone asked me what was my greatest memory of the big man, and I said it was the many yarns he shared about living in Sydney during the underworld days, and his bellowing pitched laugh. I will always hold my memories of Arthur Beetson close, and I am not ashamed to say I shed a tear every year during rugby league's State of Origin when they show Beetson smacking his club teammate, who was on the opposing team, around the ears, which captures State of Origin in one image.

Arty was a truly wonderful man. Even though we were both involved in rugby league, Beetso and I rarely talked about football. Instead, we talked about life, card games with his mates, the hotels he used to manage and, funnily enough, boxing. Beetso had a real interest in and passion for boxing. Beetso watched me, both as a kid and an adult, play in countless league games, but I was most proud when he came to watch me in my third professional fight.

Beetso rarely got angry, and I only saw his temper rear its head on one occasion, when we had a small disagreement. When he was angry, he had a bellowing voice to go with his huge stature. Out of those who knew Artie well, only a few heard his bellowing angry voice, while many more heard his child-like giggle of a laugh.

It was only at his funeral in Redcliffe, Queensland, that I saw some footage of Beetso playing, and he was exceptional. I didn't learn till later that he also was the first Indigenous Australian to be the captain of Australia in any sport.

As well as regarding Beetso as a father figure, I also consider his sons, Mark, Brad, Scott and Kristian as brothers. I still see them both at various events and always chat about the old man.

Arthur was like a second father to me. But I think the most important thing I learned from him was to tell it how it is — tell the truth. If I didn't play well or my attitude was off, Arthur let me know. He was a great man, and I miss him dearly.

JOHNNY LEWIS

Johnny Lewis has been major figure in my life and a great mentor. Though very quiet by nature and with an unforgettable softness in his voice, Johnny also shows love and care towards every boxer, not just the ones he trains. Whether it's when he's in the ring, and he'll be saying: 'Joey, I love ya, son. Box smart and be safe,' or when he finishes off a phone call with 'Joey, give my love to Mum and Dad, mate. I love ya, son,' the man is filled with love and emotion.

Once, when he was taping my hands I noticed he'd put a cross on each hand with tape. 'Is that a special way to tape your hands, Johnny?' I had asked.

'I put a cross on each hand, mate, one for you and one for the guy in the other corner. Although I want to see you win, I want the both of you to come out alive and well.'

I felt honoured and lucky when his beautiful wife, Ingrid, asked me to play guitar and sing at his surprise seventieth birthday party. Even after all these years, Johnny and I regularly call each other to check in and make sure all is well.

Johnny taught me that, with hard work and a bit of luck, anything is possible. I've heard many say that, when you have Johnny Lewis in your corner, it doesn't matter who's across on the other side of the ring, because Johnny makes you believe you could beat anyone. He's a great man with amazing motivational capabilities.

DAVID PEACHEY

As a kid, I'd always admired Indigenous NRL player David Peachey. After I played my debut first-grade NRL game against him, I followed his career even more closely.

We blackfullas tend to be drawn to each other, so when Dave signed to play with Souths when I was there, we connected immediately. Dave had a great deal of experience away from rugby league, and it was through his mentoring that I learned how to network with potential sponsors and people I could partner with in a work environment. Dave also walked me through a tough period in my life when I broke up with Brodi and Phoenix's mother, Suzie.

Dave and I are still very close today, some ten years after we played together at the Rabbitohs. Dave taught me the importance of developing kids in rugby league and giving back to the community. Dave was forever checking dates in his diary to see if he was available for a function, and is always doing his best to give back to the people, which I am forever grateful for.

WRAP-UP

- A mentor is someone who can teach you something in life or help you in an area of your life.

- Mentors are often older, because they have more lived experience.

- A mentor sets a positive example and is available to help you when you need help.

- Find a mentor or mentors who you can trust and look up to.

BE A MENTOR AND GIVE BACK

Having the good fortune to have learned some valuable life lessons from such great people, I've tried to share what I've learned by mentoring others.

Mentors have been so important to me, and now mentoring others has become a major part of my life and is something I enjoy. The way I see it, everything I've gone through has helped shape the man I have become. So if I can learn something from every one of my experiences, I can store that knowledge in my back pocket to share with others who might need some mentoring.

I take immense pride in being a mentor. It means someone values my experience and advice, and that I'm seen as someone who is willing to help people by sharing what I've learned. One of the most important mentoring roles I've had was with Steve 'Slip' Morris, a man I now consider to be one of my closest friends and a brother.

I try to help people through tough times. I always offer my help to anyone who needs it, again because of the way I was raised and the compassion I feel towards others. I've learned on my journey to always treat people well, because most people are fighting their own battles that we know nothing about.

If you model positive behaviours, you can be a mentor. But if you're also actively making some poor choices in your behaviours and lifestyle, it's hard to call yourself a mentor or role model. That's because, when you're modelling positive behaviours, any negative behaviours you also have tend to stand out.

For me, being seen as a mentor is a compliment of the highest order. It means people are noticing my positive behaviours and want me to share them. I know it has also had a positive effect on my own wellbeing. So do volunteering and fundraising, which are other good ways to give back to others. Volunteering and fundraising take compassion and remind me to be grateful for what I have and what I can do.

Being a mentor and giving back allows me to share my experiences. But they also keep me on track, because to mentor or help someone, you have to be sure your own behaviours are positive.

WRAP-uP

- Give back by being a positive role model every day.

- You can also give back by volunteering or fundraising, or always being available to help others.

- Giving back or helping out has a positive effect on your own wellbeing.

LAST WORD

There's a dark side of me, that even I can't understand.

This is a line in a song by Australian country music star Troy Cassar-Daley, called 'Yesterday's Bed', which I can really relate to. The one thing I know for sure is that I am so much more resilient and mentally tough and I am able to combat that dark side now. I still get tested every single day by deep fears that continue to haunt me, but every day is a fresh start to build on what I encountered the day before.

These days, I get to open my eyes and attack the world head on. I try to make every post a winner. I am still faced with some extremely tough situations mentally, but every day of this journey I try to be the best person I can be, and someone my kids will be proud of.

One thing I've learned to put into practice every day, during good times and bad, is to leave the negative days behind me. 'We can't change the past, only learn from it' is a good motto to live by. I do my best to learn from every negative day I have, so I can turn it into a positive if a similar situation arises.

Learn from each day. And wherever your wellbeing is at when you wake, BUILD ON THAT.

ACKNOWLEDGEMENTS

Thank you to Courtney Merritt. The way Courtney cares for all of my children, not just her biological children, Ari and Franki, reminds me why I love her so much. We have been together for a few years now, and she's still the same warm, loving, caring woman I met, a woman who puts everyone before herself.

My children and Courtney mean the world to me, and I wish my kids could wake up in the same house as me every day. But I am just so happy and so thankful that all five of my children — Brodi, Phoenix, Rome, Ari and Franki — love and adore each other, so that, despite growing up in three separate households, they have a staunch bond. Ari is growing up to be cheeky like his big sister, Phoenix, while Brodi and Rome have softer, caring personalities — but all five are thick as thieves. So to my five children, Brodi, Phoenix, Rome, Ari and Franki — I am already so proud of your journey. You are the reason I wake up every day.

I give special thanks to my parents for nurturing me, raising me and leading me to being the man I have become.

To my sisters and older brother — the memories we share of growing up I will never forget.

And to every single person I have met, loved and argued with — you have all played a part in shaping the person I am today.

Yindyamarra-bu Mandang Guwu (Respect and thank you).

GLOSSARY

Addiction: A physical or psychological need for a substance (e.g. alcohol, cocaine, nicotine) or activity (e.g. gambling, shopping) that becomes compulsive and is very difficult or impossible to stop.

Alcoholics Anonymous: An informal fellowship of recovering alcoholics who meet to encourage each other to stay sober. In Australia, there are about 18,000 members who meet in over 1,900 local meetings spread around the country.

Anxiety: An persistent feeling of fear, stress or worry even when there is no particular reason or cause. Anxiety is the most common mental health condition in Australia.

Bipolar disorder: A mental health condition with strong changes in mood and energy. People with bipolar disorder have two distinct mood swings, between *mania* (high-energy, euphoric, overconfident, racing thought and little need for sleep) and *depression* (low mood, feelings of hopelessness, extreme sadness and lack of interest and pleasure in things).

Breathing technique: Deliberate and controlled slow, even and gentle breathing to help relive symptoms of anxiety.

Depression: A mental illness that causes feelings that may include: sadness, feeling worthless, a loss of interest in activities once enjoyed, trouble sleeping or sleeping too much and thoughts of suicide.

Discrimination: Treating someone unfairly or differently because of who they are or because they possess certain characteristics. These can include a person's race, gender, religious beliefs, sexual preference, age and physical features.

Dosage: The size or frequency of a dose of a medicine or drug.

First Nations: The diverse nations that comprise Aboriginal and Torres Strait Islander peoples, each with their own language and traditions.

Illegal drug: A drug that is subject to drug prohibition laws such as cannabis, heroin, ice, cocaine and MDMA. Legal drugs include alcohol and tobacco, and drugs prescribed by doctors.

Koori: An indigenous Australian, especially one from Victoria or southern New South Wales.

Medication: A legal drug used to prevent, treat or cure an illness.

Mental health: Good mental health is a sense of wellbeing, confidence and self-esteem. It enables us to fully enjoy and appreciate other people, day-to-day life and our environment.

Mental health counsellor: A professional who provides ongoing psychological care to people dealing with depression, mental illness, substance abuse, unhealthy relationships, and other mental and psychological issues. They may also help people who have normal cognitive processes cope with difficult life events, for example, physical illness, death of loved ones, and relationship problems or divorce.

Mental illness: A mental illness is a health problem that significantly affects how a person feels, thinks, behaves, and interacts with other people.

Mentor: A guide who shares knowledge, skills and life experience to enable another towards reaching their full potential.

Mindfulness: The conscious and deliberate direction of attention on your body, mind, and feelings in the present moment.

Murri: The Indigenous Australians of modern-day Queensland and North West New South Wales.

Narcotics Anonymous: An informal fellowship of recovering drug addicts who meet to encourage each other to stay clean.

Noongar: The Indigenous Australians of modern-day south west Western Australia.

Nunga: The Indigenous Australians of modern-day southern South Australia.

Palawa: The first nations people of Tasmania.

Panic attack: A brief episode of intense anxiety, which causes the physical sensations of fear, even when there is no actual danger.

Prescription drug: A drug that can only be taken when permitted by a doctor.

Psychologist: A psychologist is a health professional with an expertise in human behaviour. Many psychologists work directly with those experiencing difficulties, such addiction and mental health disorders including anxiety and depression.

Racism: A belief in the superiority of one race over another, which often results in discrimination and prejudice towards people based on their race or ethnicity.

Substance use disorder: When a person's use of alcohol or another drug leads to significant impairment, such as health problems, disability, and failure to meet major responsibilities at work, school, or home.

Suicide ideation: Thinking that life isn't worth living, ranging in intensity from fleeting thoughts through to well thought-out plans for killing oneself.

Wiradjuri: An Australian first nations people whose land covers a large area of central and southern New South Wales.

RESOURCES

Kids Helpline (Ages 5–25)

1800 55 1800

Kidshelpline.com.au

Kids Helpine helps young Australian's to express themselves, build confidence and live safely. Kids can chat with qualified counsellors FREE.

Lifeline

13 11 14

www.lifeline.org.au

Lifeline is a national charity providing all Australians experiencing a personal crisis with access to 24-hour crisis support and suicide prevention services. Lifeline is committed to empowering Australians to be suicide-safe through connection, compassion and hope. Lifeline's vision is for an Australia free of suicide.

Suicide Call Back Service

1300 659 467

www.suicidecallbackservice.org.au

Suicide Call Back Service provides free phone, video and counselling for anyone affected by suicide.

Blue Pages

www.bluepages.anu.edu.au/index.

Crisis services by state:

ACT

Mental Health Triage Service

(02) 6205 1065 or 1800 629 354

NSW

Mental Health Help Line

1800 011 511

NT

Northern Territory Crisis & Assessment Telephone Triage and Liaison Service

1800 682 288 (1800 NT CATT)

QLD
Health Advice
13 43 25 84 (13 HEALTH)

SA
Assessment & Crisis Intervention Service
131 465

TAS
Mental Health Services Helpline
1800 332 388

VIC
Suicide Line
1300 651 251

WA
WA Mental Health Emergency Response Line
1300 555 788 (Metro area)
1800 676 822 (Peel area)

Crisis Care Helpline
1800 199 008

INDIGENOUS MENTAL HEALTH

The Enemy Within: Suicide Prevention & Wellbeing Education
www.joewilliams.com.au

Social and Emotional Wellbeing and Mental Health Services in Aboriginal Australia
www.sewbmh.org.au

Head to Health
www.headtohealth.gov.au/supporting-yourself/
support-for/aboriginal-and-torres-strait-islander-
peoples
A great site to access holistic health support.

MENTAL HEALTH – GENERAL

beyondblue
1300 22 46 36
www.beyondblue.org.au
www.beyondblue.org.au/who-does-it-affect/
aboriginal-and-torres-strait-islander-people

beyondblue provides information and support to help everyone in Australia achieve their best possible mental health, whatever their age and wherever they live.

Black Dog Institute

www.blackdoginstitute.org.au/

The Black Dog Institute is dedicated to understanding, preventing and treating mental illness. It is about creating a world where mental illness is treated with the same level of concern, immediacy and seriousness as physical illness; where scientists work to discover the causes of illness and new treatments, and where discoveries are immediately put into practice through health services, technology and community education.

Headspace (for young Australians)

1800 650 890

www.headspace.org.au

Headspace is the National Youth Mental Health Foundation providing early intervention mental health services to 12–25 year olds, along with assistance in promoting young peoples' wellbeing. This covers four core areas: mental health, physical health, work and study support and alcohol and other drug services.

Head to Health

www.headtohealth.gov.au

www.headtohealth.gov.au/supporting-yourself/
support-for/aboriginal-and-torres-strait-islander-
peoples

A great site to access holistic health support.

MensLine Australia

1300 78 99 78

www.mensline.org.au

MensLine Australia is a telephone and online
counselling service for men with family and
relationship concerns. Mensline is there to help
anywhere, anytime.

RuralLink

Specialist after-hours mental health telephone service
for people in rural communities of Western Australia
1800 552 002

ALCOHOL AND DRUG SUPPORT SERVICES

Australian Drug Information Network

www.adin.com.au

Head to Health

www.headtohealth.gov.au

Healthdirect

www.healthdirect.gov.au/drug-and-alcohol-rehabilitation

The Council for Aboriginal Alcohol Program Services (CAAPS) Aboriginal Corporation (NT)

www.caaps.org.au

The Council for Aboriginal Alcohol Program Services (CAAPS) Aboriginal Corporation is the largest not-for-profit family-focused residential alcohol and other drug rehabilitation centre in Northern Australia. In addition to rehabilitation, we provide community members support for appropriate referrals and work to prevent homelessness.

Wungening Aboriginal Corporation (Western Australia)

www.wungening.com.au/

Podcasts

soberpodcasts.com

CHRONIC TRAUMATIC ENCEPHALOPATHY (CTE)

concussionfoundation.org/CTE-resources/what-is-CTE
www.bu.edu/cte/about/frequently-asked-questions
www.mja.com.au/journal/2012/196/9/does-football-cause-brain-damage

MINDFULNESS RESOURCES

Online

au.reachout.com/articles/how-to-practice-mindfulness
sydney.edu.au/students/health-and-wellbeing/mindfulness-and-relaxation.html

Books

Sarah Edelman, *Change Your Thinking*
Sarah Edelman, *Good Thinking*
Thich Nhat Hanh, *The Miracle of Mindfulness*